architecture on sports facilities

SPORTS FACILITIES

Edition 2005

Author: Carles Broto
Publisher: Arian Mostaedi
Editorial Coordinator: Jacobo Krauel
Architectural Advisor: Pilar Chueca
Graphic designer & production: Marta Rojals, Pilar Chueca
Text: contributed by the architects,
    edited by Marta Rojals, Núria Rodríguez
English Translation: Núria Rodríguez

Cover photograph: ©Bitter Bredt Fotografie

© Carles Broto i Comerma
Jonqueres, 10, 1-5
08003 Barcelona, Spain
Tel.: +34 93 301 21 99
 Fax: +34-93-301 00 21
E-mail: info@linksbooks.net
www. linksbooks.net

ISBN 84-934007-7-7

Printed in China

architecture on sports facilities

structure

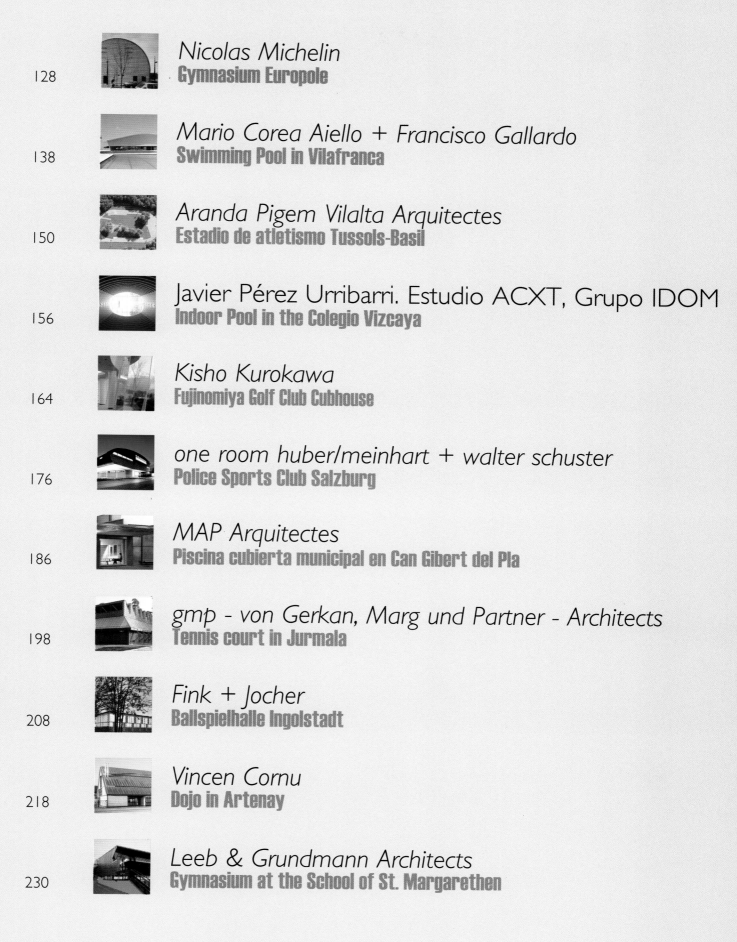

INTRODUCTION

There is no doubt that sport, in all its different manifestations, is one of the most widespread and popular cultural expressions throughout the world. Practiced by civilizations through the ages, sport is a pastime intrinsic to human nature. From ancient civilizations to the present day, it has included everything from primitive games focused on competition and dominating nature to the complexity of sporting events in our times, events which have transformed into social, economic and cultural phenomena in themselves.

At present, and with increasing frequency, sporting activities are giving rise to a multiplicity of infrastructures designed for practicing and enjoying sports, many of them directly related to the increasing professionalization of sport and its ability to reach massive audiences through communications technology. At the same time, the increasing visibility of sport in society is creating a more "domestic" need for various small-scale sports spaces that can respond to the leisure needs of citizens of all ages and descriptions.

In order to reflect the range of different expressions covered by sports architecture, the pages that follow offer a compilation of a wide selection of installations, indoor and outdoor, public and private, located in both rural and urban environments, from small clubs and school gymnasiums to sports complexes and large stadiums. In addition to formal and expressive qualities, the architects of all these projects also share a special interest in exploring alternative ways of dealing with the ever-present requirements of sporting regulations, finding ways to avoid the shadow that standardization tends to cast over these kinds of infrastructures.

Whether they use the most innovative or the most traditional techniques, all of the designs included in this book offer new - and often surprising - aesthetics, which are sure to serve as inspiration for many future projects. And then stories, big and small, will follow: the architects' hand gives way to competitions and tournaments, training and entertainment, moments of relaxation at the swimming pool, anonymous school championships and big afternoons at the football.... Architecture that, in the end, creates a space for the thousands of manifestations of sporting values which reflect, as they have in the past and will continue to do in the future, a society's values at each moment in history.

NO.MAD Arquitectos

Lasesarre Soccer Stadium

Barakaldo, Spain

Photographs: Roland Halbe / ARTUR

It is difficult to build in tune with nature: history is full of confrontations between man and nature, and man's ability to imitate it has always been coarse and limited. This stadium, however, approaches the problem by trying to create a sensitive kind of camouflage through the use of the variations of sunlight in a forest - as in the thousand and one trees planted next to the building - but using artificial-natural vibrant aluminum below the folds of the canopies.

The entrances, through this fictitious natural-vegetation wall, transport visitors to a new geography, one that controls the flow and placement of spectators. The architects have defined an expressive exterior and an emblematic interior made up of multiple individual "buildings" separated from each other by the folds in the grandstand, their individual gardens and the different ways of seeing. The building only shuts down for one and a half hours per week, and it invites users to imagine other uses, based on the idea that a stadium is not just for sport. The many different modules are unified by the roof, which directly reflects the layout of the grandstands. It allows the soft northern light to permeate the interior, and cut-out sections let the rain into the inner gardens. At night, the building becomes an enormous lamp, like a glowing natural element in the landscape.

The grandstands were erected over the ruins of blast furnaces, and the foundations, made of stainless steel-cased micropiles, cross the contaminated sludge surrounding the Nervión estuary. In order to avoid visible braces or other revealing structures, over a million kilos of steel was used, with different shapes screwed in, reinforced steel of diverse forms and thickness. The prefabricated elements, assembled in a little over a month, are the perfect solution for emergency situations, solid, resistant and not at all versatile.

The pipes used in the installations travel through a ring tunnel so that they cannot be seen, though they can be controlled. The cutting-edge lighting fixtures are also hidden, adapting to the geometry of the folds and cutouts, sketching the skeleton of the building in the darkness. One hundred and fifty projectors with adjustable light cones were installed in the stadium to be used in the future for digital TV.

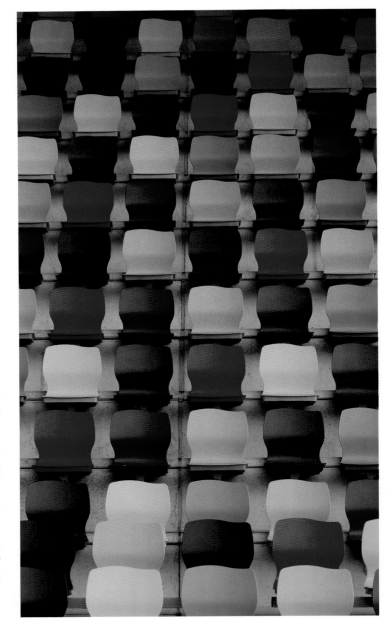

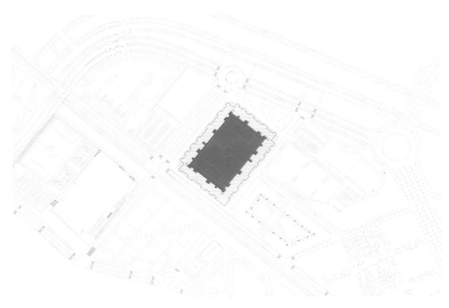

The exterior is an expressive single form, which is made up of various independent "buildings" separated from each other by the folds of the grandstands. Each of them contains its own individual services and entrances, which makes it possible for them to be used independently.

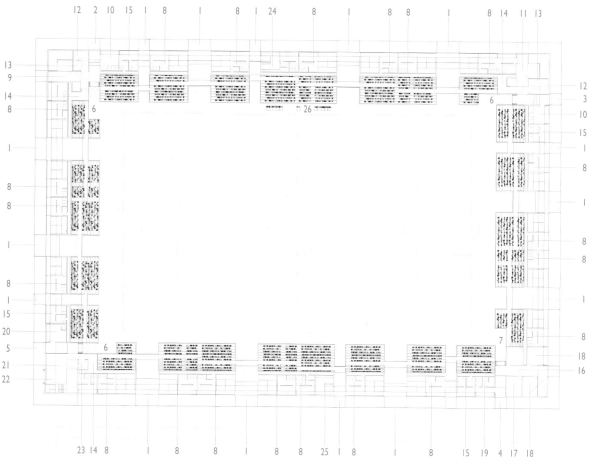

1. Spectators entrance
2. Visiting team and referee entrance
3. Barakaldo F.C. players entry
4. Vehicle access
5. Entrance to municipal club and cafeteria
6. Entrance to the field
7. Vehicle access to the field
8. Spectators' bathrooms
9. Visiting team locker room
10. Referee locker room
11. Barakaldo F.C. locker room
12. Medical examination room
13. Drug testing room
14. Equipment area
15. Disabled bathrooms
16. Truck loading bay
17. Materials storage area
18. Facilities
19. Staff locker rooms
20. Barakaldo F.C. security and control office
21. Municipal club and cafeteria
22. Ticket offices
23. Kitchen
24. VIP area
25. Technical retransmission area
26. Benches

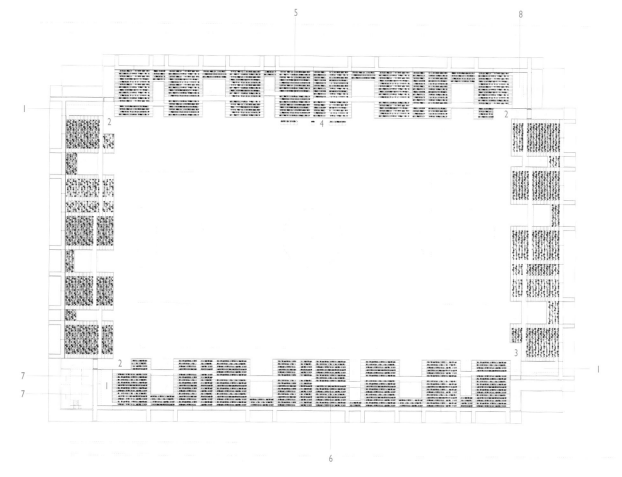

1. Rest area and external bar
2. Field services and player entrances
3. Vehicle access to field
4. Benches
5. VIP seating
6. Retransmission area
7. Barakaldo F. C. administrative offices

The cutting-edge lighting fixtures are concealed by the geometry of the folds, and define the skeleton of the entire building in the darkness.

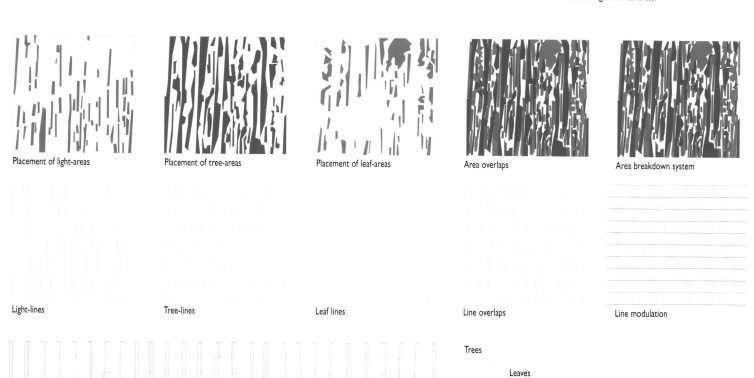

Placement of light-areas

Placement of tree-areas

Placement of leaf-areas

Area overlaps

Area breakdown system

Light-lines

Tree-lines

Leaf lines

Line overlaps

Line modulation

Trees

Leaves

Light

Translation to louvers of light, trees, leaves

"....What better way to create a permeable space, with no fixed size, than to imitate the wisdom of the forest? Its light, the shifting shadows as the natural light changes through the day and night. The facade tends towards depth, movement, to vibrate with the wind...a facade that aligns the exterior with the natural grove in the square adjacent to the stadium. A filter for entering another nature. The only one."

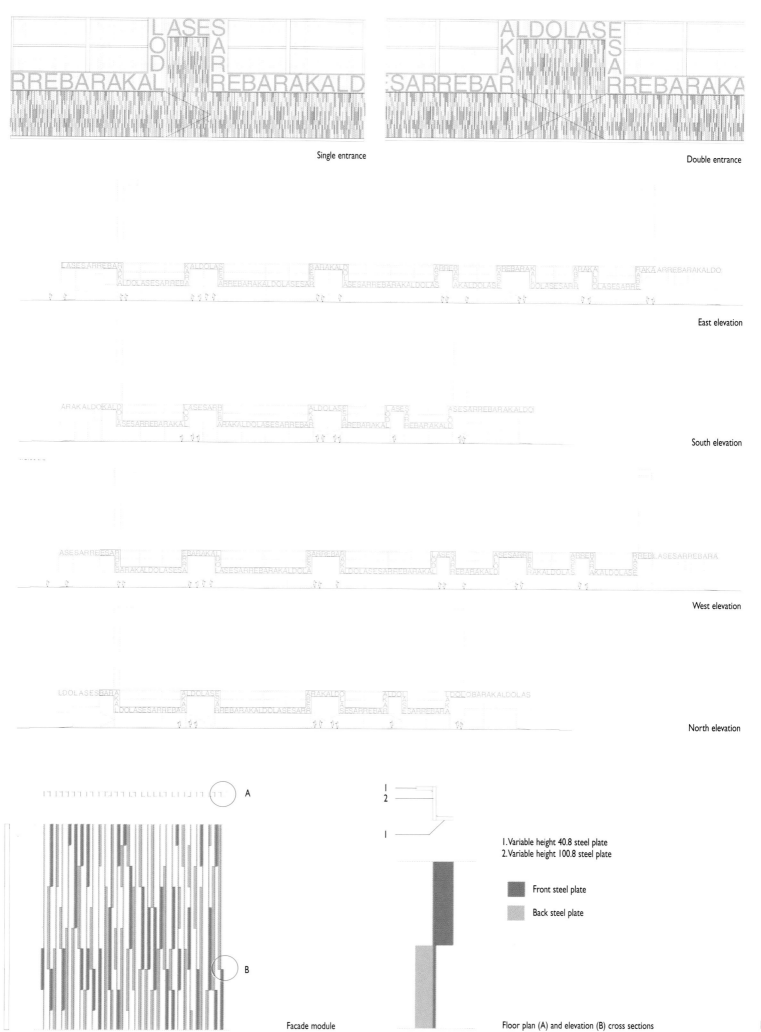

Single entrance

Double entrance

East elevation

South elevation

West elevation

North elevation

Facade module

1. Variable height 40.8 steel plate
2. Variable height 100.8 steel plate

Front steel plate

Back steel plate

Floor plan (A) and elevation (B) cross sections

15

Longitudinal section

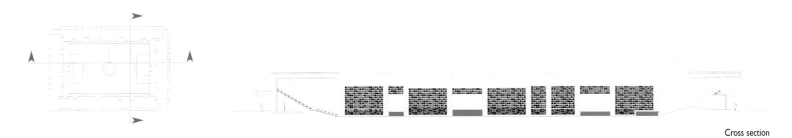

Cross section

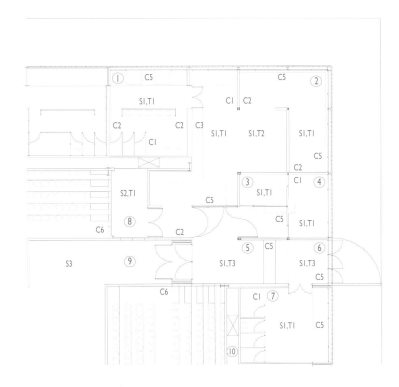

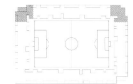

1. Visiting team bathrooms
2. Showers
3. Drug testing room
4. Medical examination room
5. Waiting room
6. Visiting players and referees entrance
7. Referee locker rooms
8. Facilities
9. Entrance to the field
10. Facilities gallery

Floors:
S1. Continuous self-leveling mortar resin floor with transparent polyurethane resin finish.
S2. Stairs with cement-glued artificial turf over concrete slab.

Ceilings:
T1. Continuous KNAUF plaster ceiling with plastic paint finish.
T2. Ipe wood strips for exteriors.
T3. Extended steel grille of pre-galvanized steel treated for marine protection and lacquered.

Walls:
C1. Single freestanding KNAUF partition with smooth plastic paint finish.
C2. Single freestanding KNAUF partition finished with Gresite carpet tiles.
C3. Ipe wood strips for exteriors.
C4. Laminated mirror glued to base.
C5. Laminated transparent Climalit glass.
C6. Prefabricated concrete panels, polished and sealed.

The colored seats are like a wink at the masculine culture surrounding soccer, an irony that mixes colors as though it were mixing the population itself.

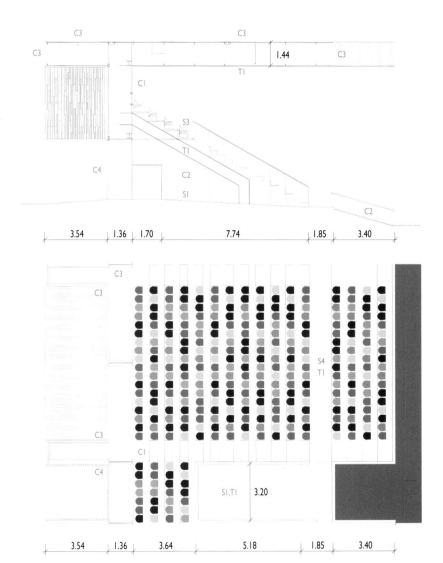

Floors:
      S1. Continuous self-leveling mortar resin floor with transparent polyurethane resin finish.
      S2. Continuous polished concrete floor.
      S3. Prefabricated polished and sealed prefabricated elements.
      S3. Steel plate embedded in resin floor.

Ceilings:
      T1. Extended steel grille of pre-galvanized steel treated for marine protection and lacquered.
      T2. Continuous KNAUF 47 plaster ceiling with smooth plastic paint finish.

Walls:
      C1. Extended steel grille of pre-galvanized steel treated for marine protection and lacquered.
      C2. Extended steel grille of pre-galvanized steel treated for marine protection and lacquered and trimmed
          with steel sheet.
      C3. White "Sunmodul"-type cellular polycarbonate on plastified pieces.
      C4. Facade of painted steel modules.

Zaha Hadid

Bergisel Ski Jump

Innsbruck, Austria

Photographs: Hélène Binet

In December 1999, Zaha Hadid architects won an International Competition to design a new ski jump on Bergisel Mountain in Innsbruck, a city with a long tradition as a venue for winter sport competitions. The new ski jump is part of a larger refurbishment project for the Olympic arena and replaces the old ski jump, which no longer met international standards.

The project is unusual because it went beyond the relatively one-dimensional task of designing a technical building for a single purpose. The striking silhouette is what made Hadid's design stand out from the others: suggesting an almost animal-like presence, the ski jump has all the hallmarks to become a local landmark. About 90 meters high and almost 50 meters long, the building is a combination of a tower and a bridge. Structurally, it is divided into a vertical concrete tower and a spatial green structure, which integrates the ramp and the cafe. Two lifts take visitors up to the cafe 40 meters above the peak of Bergisel, where spectators enjoy views over a spectacular alpine panorama, and watch the athletes below flying across the Innsbruck skyline.

The design was complicated by the coexistence of underground, surface and aerial construction. To coordinate the construction process, the architects needed to set up precise logistics on the building site, taking into consideration the difficult topographical conditions of the mountain and the high technical demands of the building, while working within a short construction schedule.

Conceptually, the structural elements are not different systems, just part of an overall construction that came together to form a uniform, fluid building. To support this image of fluidity, the building was covered with metal sheets marked with fine vertical grooves that follow the curves and reflect light differently according to the time of day, while at night, lights trace the cafe and the track of the ramp. The inside of the ramp, which has a U-shaped cross section, and the inside of the cafe are lit by strips of light that change color.

The new Bergisel Ski Jump is a sweeping, geometric run that fits perfectly against the background of the towering Alps.

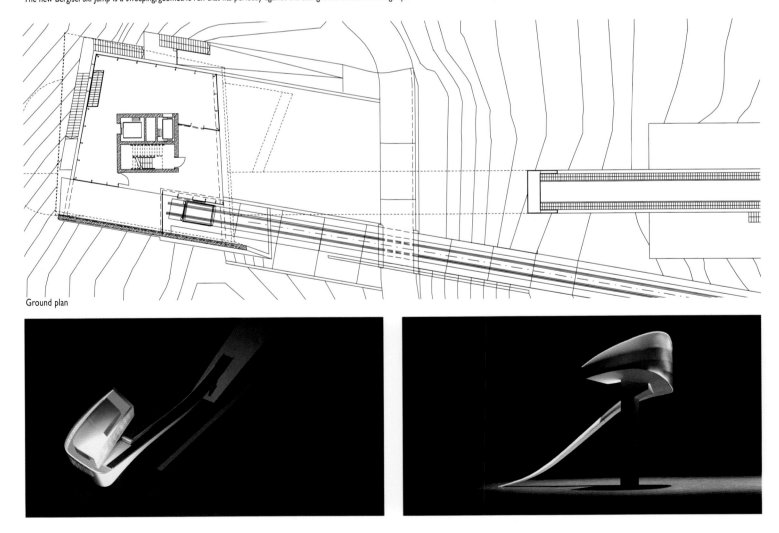

Ground plan

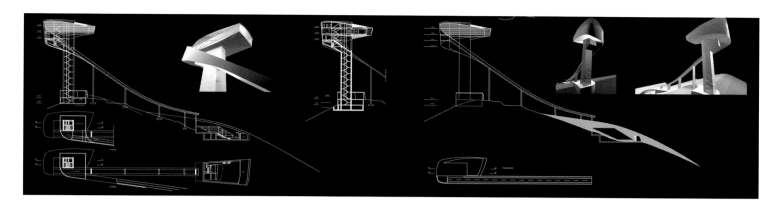

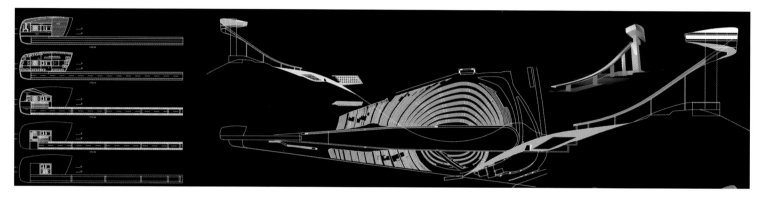

The brief called for a hybrid between specialized sports facility and public areas including a cafe and a viewing terrace, expressed by the architects as a single new shape that extends the topography of the slope into the sky.

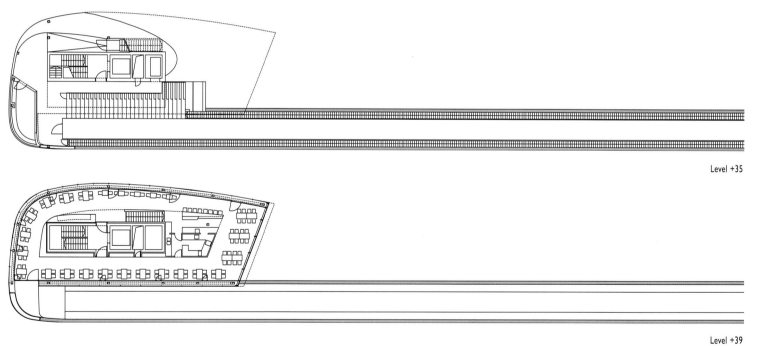

Level +35

Level +39

Level +43

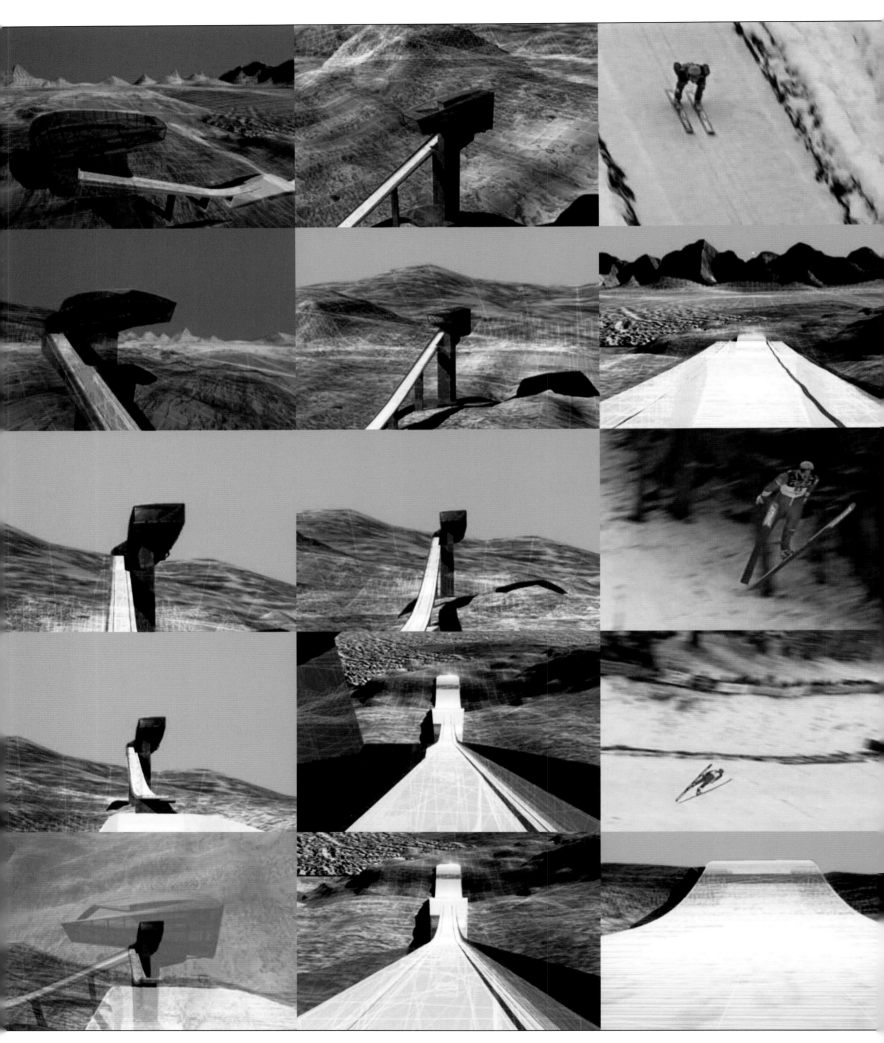

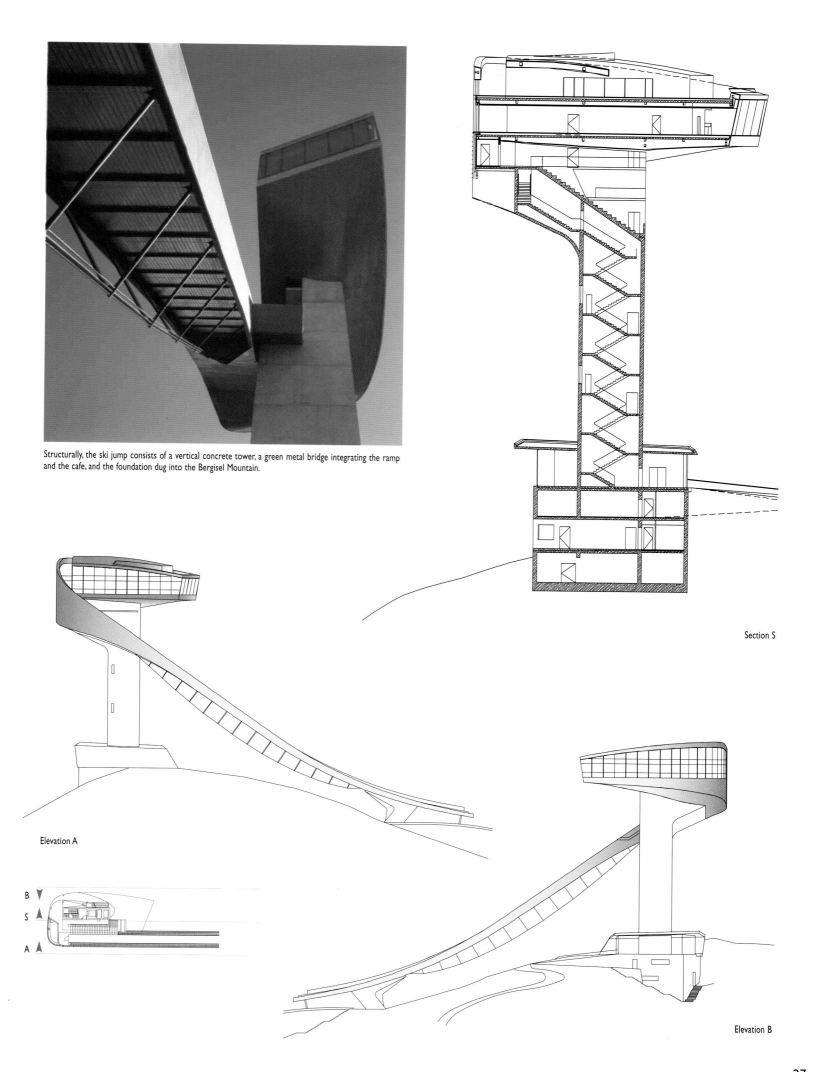

Structurally, the ski jump consists of a vertical concrete tower, a green metal bridge integrating the ramp and the cafe, and the foundation dug into the Bergisel Mountain.

Section S

Elevation A

B

S

A

Elevation B

The building was covered with metal sheets marked with fine vertical grooves that follow the curves and reflect light differently according to the time of day, while at night, lights trace the cafe and the track of the ramp.

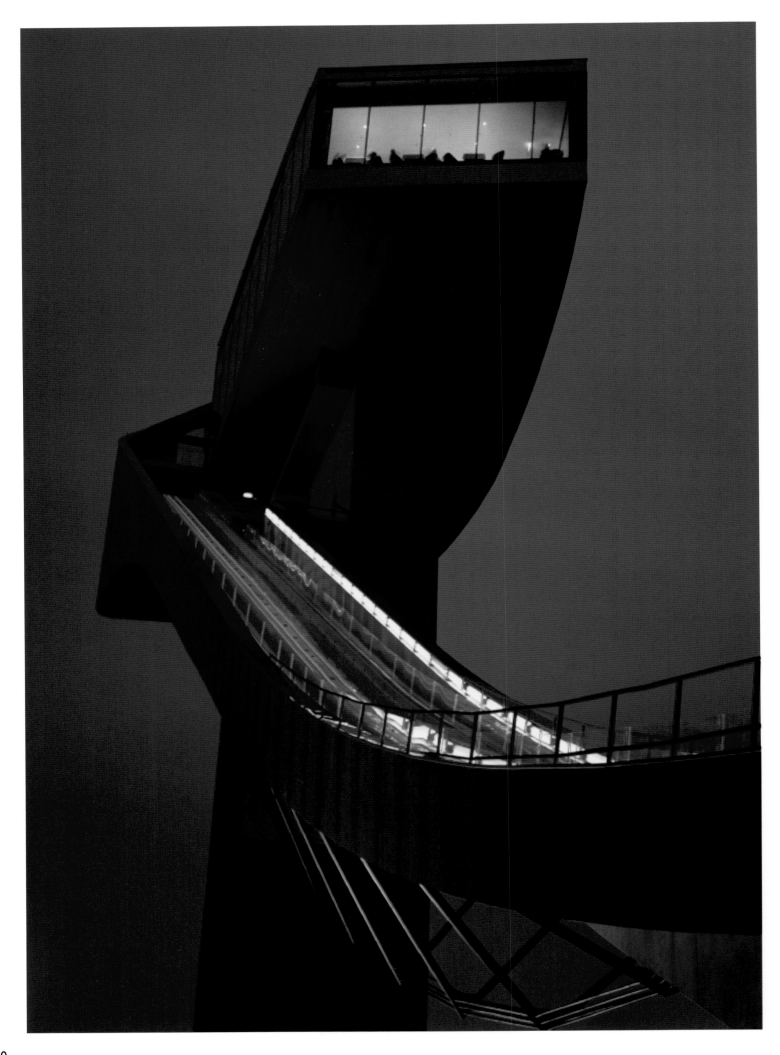

Langhof ®

Sports complex for performing artists

Berlin, Germany

Photographs: Bitter Bredt Fotografie

Permanent buildings for performing artists are something of a rarity, and this was particularly the case with the training and presentation facilities of Germany's only state school of circus and variety arts. Founded in 1956 in East Berlin before merging with Berlin's Staatliche Ballettschule (State School of Ballet), it lacked its own, permanent hall. To address this problem, the Senate Administration for Urban Development organized an architectural competition with a limited number of participants in 1995, and awarded the first prize to LANGHOF® studio.

Basing his design on the specific needs of the artists, Chirstoph Langhof created and integral, generously proportioned room with staggered ceiling heights for the different exercises. All the secondary functions such as changing rooms, seminar rooms and ballet studios were concentrated in a single adjacent building.

Through architectonic artistry - by manipulating geometry and light - a cloak of glowing warmth was created, a functional and inspirational space that radiates equal measures of dynamism, calm and poise. The space was designed to be entirely flexible and free of supports.

The choice of a multi-layer type of construction reflects the architect's commitment to sustainability and energy efficiency: the multi-layer construction of the hall regulates the interior climate, adjusting to temperature extremes in both summer and winter, and significantly reduces the need for artificial light. The generous dimensions of the indoor space are reflected outside in the large structural shape of similarly generous design. This was achieved by stretching a translucent membrane of PTFE glass fiber cloth over a vast curved structure made of wood glue trusses that, in combination with the mortises and the inner skin of the building, provides entirely glare-free daytime lighting.

With its textile membrane, the wood of the arch binders and glazed white wooden lamellae, which reflect the staggered shape of the interior, the building fits into its rather disjointed urban context without the slightest attempt at dominance. Instead, through its unobtrusiveness and its emphasis on light materials, it provides a new focus for its context. It is a natural building using modern and functional architecture that is also sensual and capable of translating complex requirements into a convincing space. A house for flying, for countless moments of weightless physics and sharpened spatial perception, and which provides the School for Artistry with a home that fulfils their training and performance needs in an efficient, ambitious way, and in an unmistakable and distinctive atmosphere.

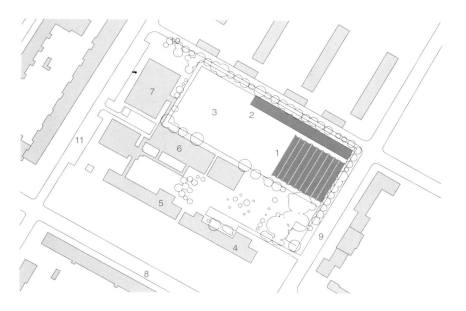

Siteplan

 1. Sport hall
 2. Locker rooms buildings
 3. External activity space
 4. Primary school
 5. Administrative building
 6. State school of ballet and of circus and variety artistry
 8. Erich-Weinert-Strasse
 9. Hosermann Strasse
10. Schieritz Strasse
11. Gubitz Strasse

Groundfloor

 1. Sports hall
 2. Auditorium
 3. Toilets
 4. Jumping pit
 5. Equipament room
 6. Control room
 7. Entrance for the audience
 8. Connecting passage
 9. Corridor
10. Locker rooms, showers, toilets
11. Workshop room
12. Entrance hall
13. Main entrance
14. Plant room
15. Ballet room
16. Multipurpose room

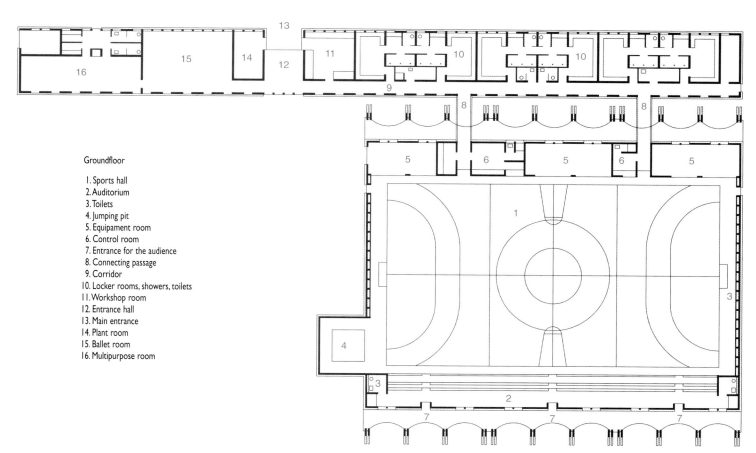

35

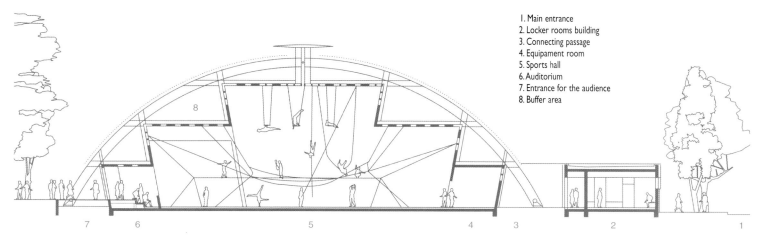

1. Main entrance
2. Locker rooms building
3. Connecting passage
4. Equipament room
5. Sports hall
6. Auditorium
7. Entrance for the audience
8. Buffer area

7 6   5   4 3   2   1

The interior walls and ceilings are suspended from an arch-binder construction and set at three stages of 3.5 m, 7 m and up to 11 m.

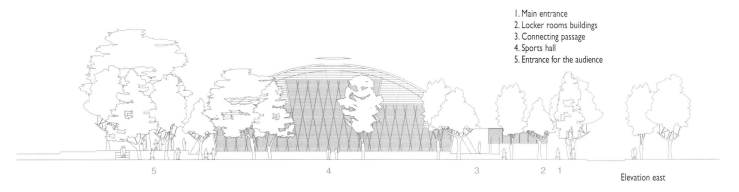

1. Main entrance
2. Locker rooms buildings
3. Connecting passage
4. Sports hall
5. Entrance for the audience

5   4   3   2 1

Elevation east

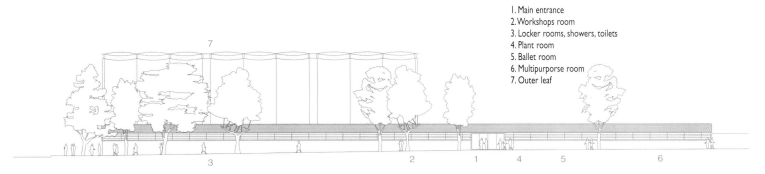

1. Main entrance
2. Workshops room
3. Locker rooms, showers, toilets
4. Plant room
5. Ballet room
6. Multipurporse room
7. Outer leaf

3   2 1 4 5   6

Elevation north

37

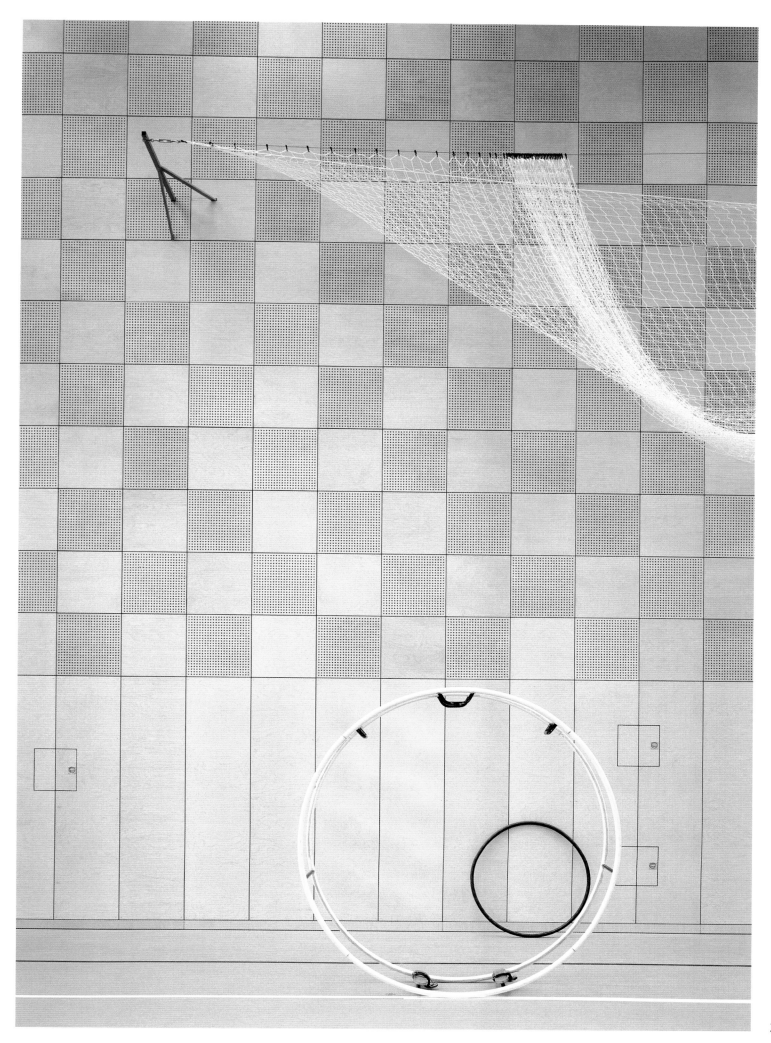

The heavily structured paneling made of warmly shimmering Birchwood panels contributes to the impression of the hall as a unique spatial experience.

Rue Royale Architectes

Balloon Box

Francheville, France

Photographs: Michel Goiffon

Francheville is a town located in the west of Lyon with a strong sports policy and a green area of several hectares, Le Parc des Sports, dedicated to sporting activity. This project was an opportunity to consolidate and update this park, adding new basketball and volleyball courts and giving the gymnasium access to sanitation facilities and the overall complex the consistency it lacked in terms of form and function. The idea for the Box was to create a building that would not clash with the existing buildings, which dated from the 70s and 80s, but would be striking enough to be identified as the leading building of the new complex.

The Balloon Box is a sheer parallelepiped, 30 meters long and 11 meters high. It has a metal structure and light facades: the north one is made of translucent polycarbonate and the other three are blind and coated with smooth panels.

The Box is lifted from its concrete base by a 50 centimeter glass strip that gives it lightness and magic, allowing a view over the outdoor areas and allowing natural light into the building. When night falls, the powerful lighting required by competition games illuminates the glass strip, which then makes the Box seem to lift from its base and levitate in the landscape.

Other less important volumes, with lazured concrete walls, act as a buffer between the games room and the older buildings, connecting the games room to the former buildings and housing new reception areas, sanitation facilities and technical rooms.

The entrance, which is in keeping with the size of the new complex, is marked by two five-meter high doors that have been set in one of the concrete walls, so that the rough finish acts as a backdrop for the elaborate work of the Box's façade.

The striking façades of the Balloon Box were made possible by pioneering use of the "digital print" process. Three of the exterior walls were faced with high density laminated panels, printed with a vertical garden design by the artist Laurent Vailler, inspired by the high density of vegetation surrounding the building.

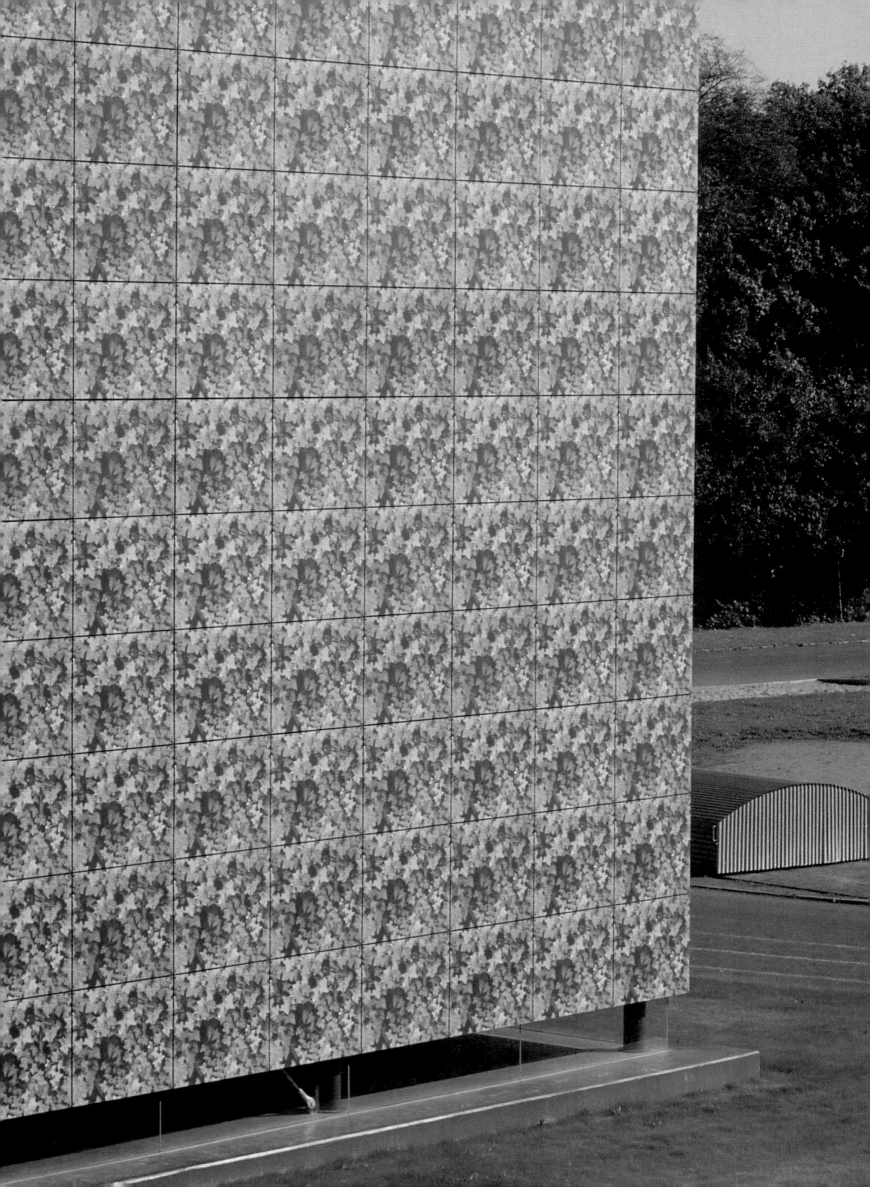

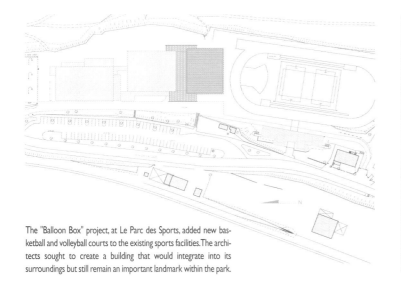

The "Balloon Box" project, at Le Parc des Sports, added new basketball and volleyball courts to the existing sports facilities. The architects sought to create a building that would integrate into its surroundings but still remain an important landmark within the park.

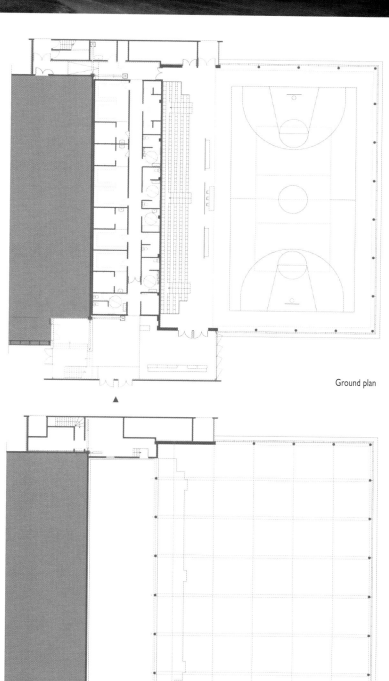

Ground plan

First plan

The "digital print" process developed by Abet Laminati allows high density laminated panels to be used for façades, which means the upper surface can be used as a base for a printed picture. The technique of four color printing which allows any design, however complex, to be reproduced, was used on a façade for the first time in Europe on the Balloon Box.

The Balloon Box is a sheer parallelepiped, 30 meters long by 11 meters high. The north façade is covered in translucent polycarbonate, while the other three are blind, and covered with smooth panels.

53

Longitudinal section

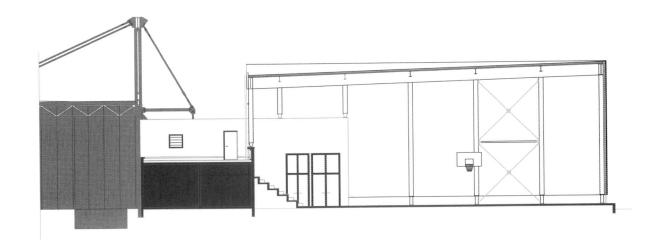

Cross section

The glass strip that separates the building from its base makes the interior space feel open, and allows spectators on the lower tiers a view of the activities taking place in the park. Because of the low height, there is no risk of excess heat or glare from the sun.

Böge Lindner Architeckten

Extension of the Wilhelmsburg School

Hamburg, Germany

Photographs: Heiner Leiska

The Wilhelmsburg integrated school is a full-time attendance school, created from the fusion between the Perlstieg and Rotenhäuser street schools. Its location, in an area of social conflict in Hamburg, means that it has to provide special support services for students. The extension project consisted of building classrooms, a sports hall and a fitness hall, providing an opportunity to connect and centralize the two school locations, and to create a building that could become a new architectural presence in that part of the city.

The linking and centralization of the schools was achieved proportionally through the new construction and the creation of an outdoor area. The unusual placement of the sports hall over the classrooms gave rise to a compact, longitudinal form on the southern side of the site, with a large area of open and flexible space between the two school buildings. This outdoor area is not just a transit zone, but also a useable space. The integration of the sport pavilion into the main building created a building of unusual proportions which, as a sculptural presence, has an almost monumental force and energy.

The abundance of light and the materials used in the two floors of classrooms and especially in the sports hall are the most important elements of the interior spaces. The fitness hall was placed over the equipment room, with a view to the sports hall and access to the roof area that can be used for outdoor exercises.

The structure of the sports hall is built from laminated wood and the glass in the skylight includes integrated lamellae to screen sunlight and prevent glare. For the same purpose, the hall's exterior glass facade is made from opaque glass. The compact nature of the building has made it possible to create a large open outdoor area between the buildings that can be used as a playground, and which integrates the existing trees.

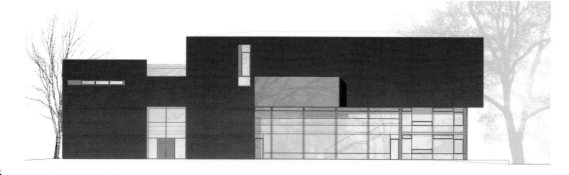

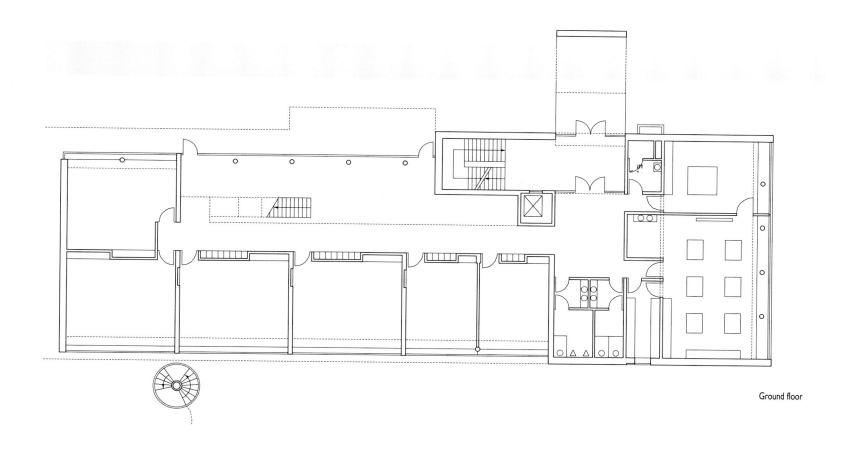

Ground floor

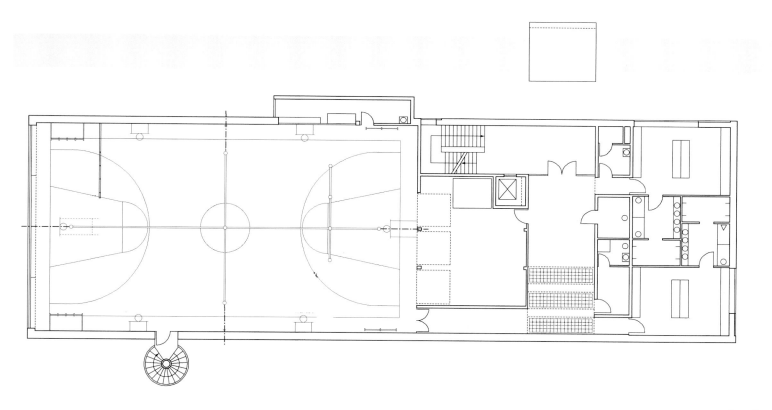

Second floor

The spaces for classrooms and the classrooms are located on ground level and on the first floor. The sports complex was placed directly over these teaching spaces, and accessed through a large freestanding stairwell.

59

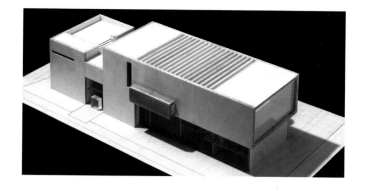

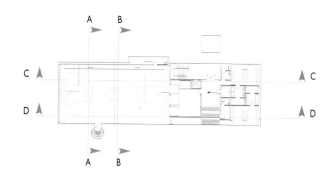

Section AA

Section BB

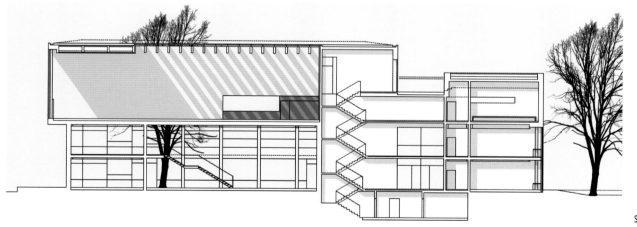

Section CC

Section DD

North elevation

South elevation

East elevation

West elevation

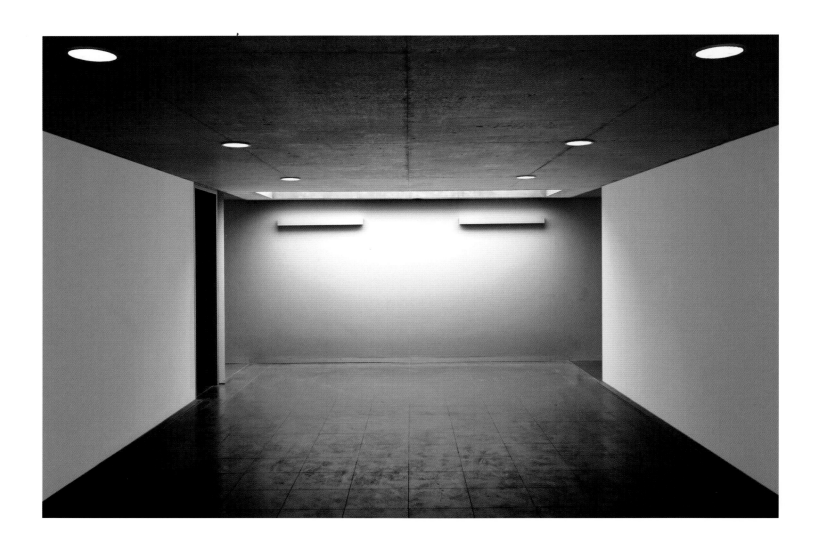

The glass of the skylights includes integrated lamellae to screen sunlight, and together with the placement of the wooden beams, achieves an optimum anti-glare effect. The external wall of the sports hall is made of opaque glass, in order to avoid unwanted glare.

Bétrix & Consolascio

Sports pavilion "In der Herti"

Zoug, France

Photographs: Guido Baselgia, Bétrix & Consolascio

Irregularly planned residential areas surround the train tracks like implants, and, in the center, there is an industrial zone with large building of various shapes. The effect is a place where built areas and open spaces flow into each other. The new pavilion was built in this context, with the building approaching the embankment and setting up a dialogue with it, although each element obeys its own laws and maintains its independence. Viewed from different points, the flat façades recall the small multicolored bits of glass in a kaleidoscope. The building's exterior skin does more than just protect the building. It is a stratification of sparkling colors that are lost in the depths, with the façades covered in glazed amethyst colored pieces. The interior of the structure cannot be read from the outside. The internal space, a nave, is surrounded by pillars supporting the large ceiling. They surround the playing area on three sides, creating a space that is almost like a perfect roman arena, in which the performances and competitions take place.

The glazing of the façades allows a diffused light to penetrate the building, but from the interior the source of the light is not obvious. To avoid the effects of direct sunlight, the building has no views to the exterior. This means that spectators are immersed in an artificial universe, emphasized and distorted by color. The pavilion is surrounded by red and yellow, increasing the reference to an arena and endowing it with a sense of open space.

The secondary training rooms on three levels and the technical equipment are embedded into the black concrete grandstand like boxes within boxes. This leaves the pavilion area free, and in spite of its multiple compartments it is perceived as a compact space.

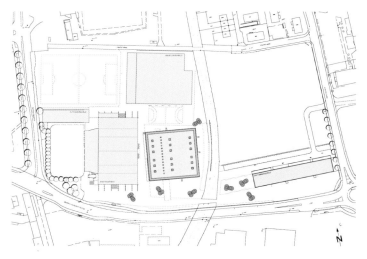

The pavilion, which is perceived as a compact space, is integrated into a context of motley residential areas adjacent to the train lines and an industrial area of irregularly shaped forms and volumes, so that there is an overall flow between built areas and open spaces.

The way the light changes throughout the day, the coloured glazing, the weather and the observer's position create almost infinite variations in the building's appearance, plays of form and color that make it appear at times cool, sometimes warm.

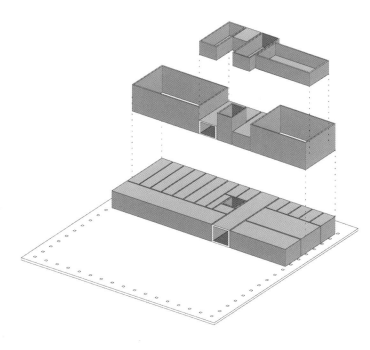

The lockers, equipment rooms and retractable grandstand are located on the lower level. On the middle level, a large platform adjacent to the playing field contains a grandstand and public areas (cafeteria) on the same side, and, across a corridor, the training rooms.

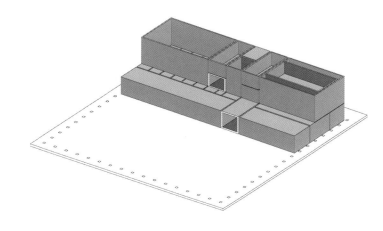

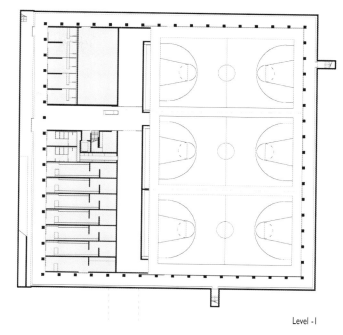

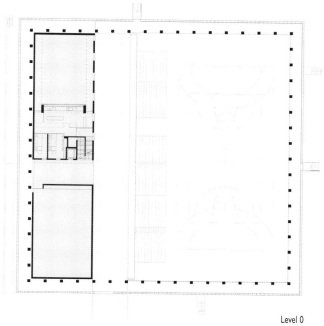

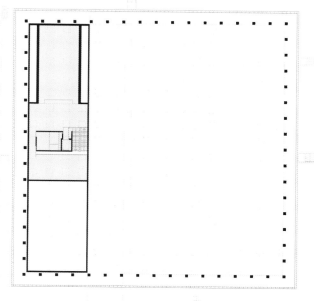

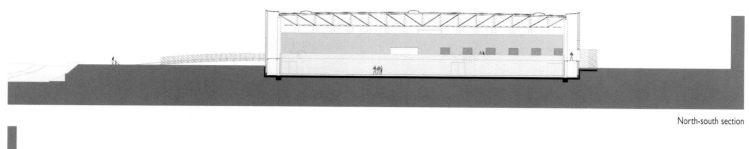

North-south section

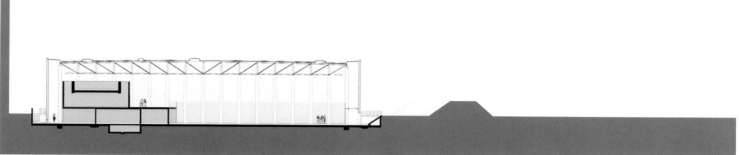

East-west section

The interior nave-like space is surrounded by pillars that support the large ceiling. These pillars surround the court on three sides, creating a kind of roman arena where the games take place.

The rooms on the intermediate and upper levels have no ceiling, so that they are acoustically interconnected.

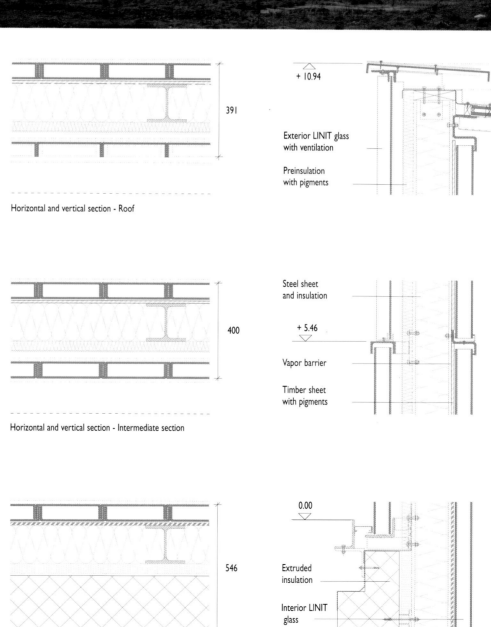

Horizontal and vertical section - Roof

+ 10.94

Exterior LINIT glass
with ventilation

Preinsulation
with pigments

391

Horizontal and vertical section - Intermediate section

Steel sheet
and insulation

+ 5.46

Vapor barrier

Timber sheet
with pigments

400

Horizontal and vertical section - Base

0.00

Extruded
insulation

Interior LINIT
glass

546

Roll & Wichert Architektur

Sports Pavilion in Bad Saulgau

Bad Saulgau, Germany

Photographs: Zooey Braun / ARTUR

The Town of Bad Saulgau, located at the rim of the "Swabian Alb" in the south of Germany, organized a design competition for a triplex sports pavilion in 2001, in order to respond to the growing demands of a sports enthusiastic community.

The aim of the competition was to develop a sports center that could be built and run at a very low cost, while still fulfilling the high standards of German sports leagues.

The town finally awarded the first prize to Roll &Wichert architects, who were engaged to carry out the design. Forced to work with restricted resources, the architects created a very dense project, blending a sports and multi-purpose hall, spectators' club and an atmospheric athletics ground with a capacity for 800 visitors. The all-embracing hall is simple and elegant in appearance, with the service and facilities scattered throughout like large pieces of furniture.

The materials used were reduced to the basics: concrete walls and pillars, 48 m long single-piece steel beams and wooden boxes and seat coverings. Rather than the usual ceramic finishes, the dressing rooms and shower cabins are finished with blue and green plastic sheets.

The highest point of the almost totally flat, sloped roof lays 10.65 meters above the field, which led the architects to excavate the lower level containing dressing and technical rooms. This allowed for a perfect view over the surrounding natural landscape from the main entrance, the mobile stands and the coffee bar.

Spectators enter the gymnasium on the public level three meters above the playfield, providing the opportunity to have a drink and relax in the lobby area while watching the game.

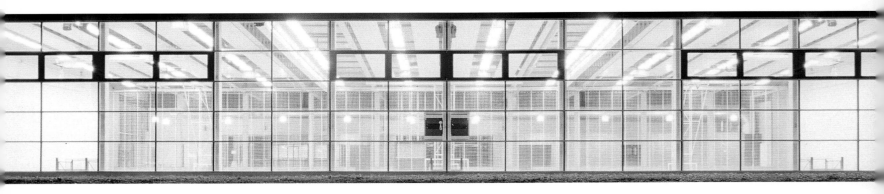

The project is a response to the need to optimize limited resources, a restriction that resulted in a compact building containing a sports complex, spectators' club and athletics track.

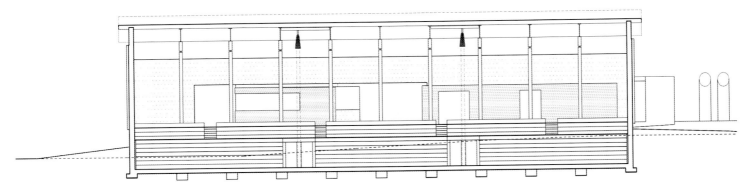

Section A-A'

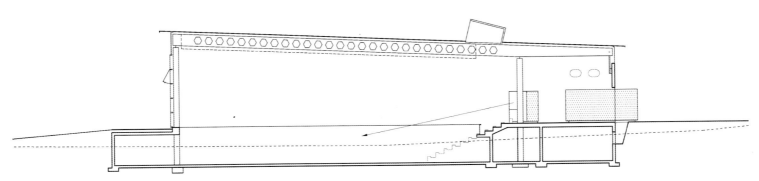

Section B-B'

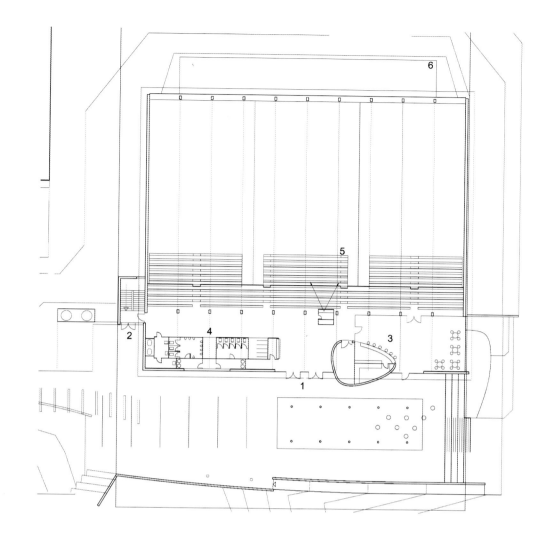

Level 0

1. Main entrance
2. Athletes entrance
3. Restaurant
4. Ticket office and services
5. Steps
6. Technical rooms

B

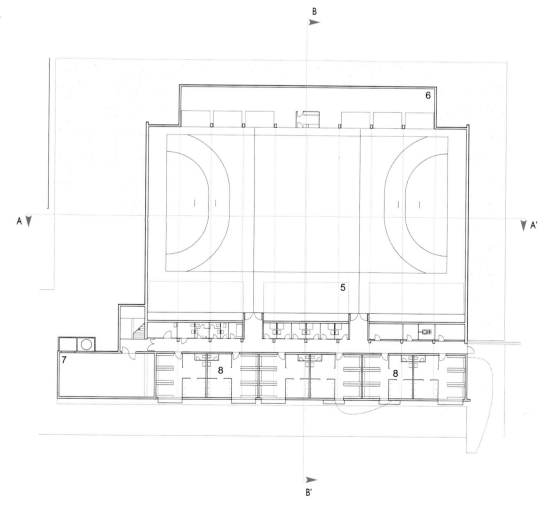

A ▼

▼ A'

Level -1

5. Steps
6. Technical rooms
7. Technil ventilation
8. Dressing rooms and showers

B'

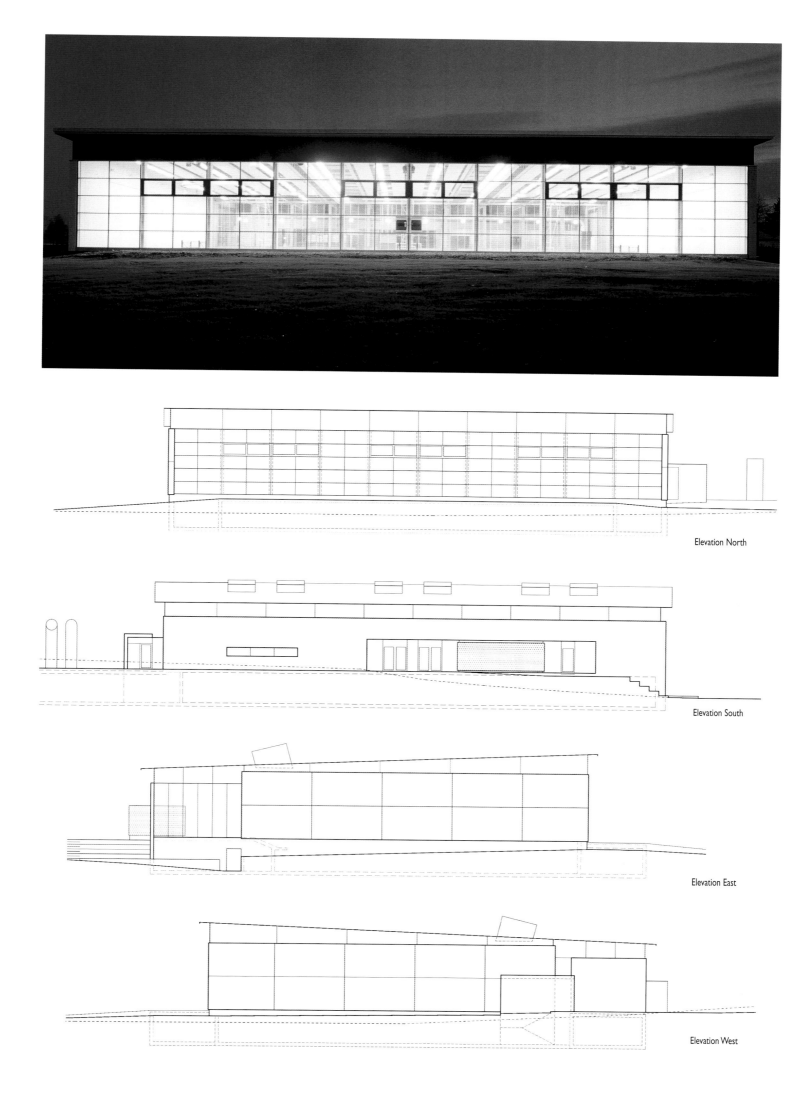

Elevation North

Elevation South

Elevation East

Elevation West

The internal layout of the pavilion, with the court, dressing rooms and technical rooms on the lower floor and the public areas three meters higher, allows spectators to visit the cafeteria and relax without missing any of the sporting action below.

The materials reflect the synthesis of the project: concrete pillars and walls, steel girders and seats and service nuclei made of wood. The wet areas have been finished with blue and green plastic sheets.

A large foyer extends through the entire length of the pavilion, housing the required services in a simple way. The wooden finishes of these service outlets bring to mind large pieces of furniture.

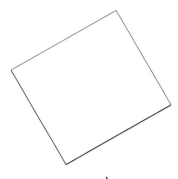

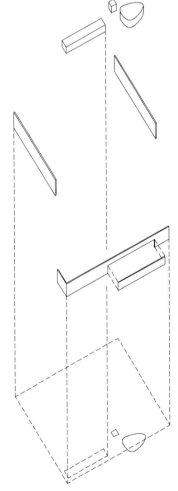

Francisco Mangado Beloqui

Indoor pool in La Coruña

La Coruña, Spain

Photographs: Roland Halbe / ARTUR

The design for this project arises from a competition that clearly requested submissions for a "prototype" building that could be built in various locations throughout the province of La Coruña. From the very beginning, the idea of a prototype was identified as a starting point of the search for a "compact" design, which led to a proposal for a building in which the longitudinal section of the single volume summarizes the functional organization of the whole. On one side is the pool, utilizing the entire height of the volume; on the other side, again making use of the total height of the section, is the gymnasium. Between the two, there is a space containing the dressing rooms and other services on the ground floor and a cafe and restaurant on the upper floor, looking over the pool and gymnasium.

The roof is, without a doubt, the element that formally identifies the building. This single, expressive element unifies everything within a single line, and is completely in keeping with the desire for a compact design. But its meaning goes beyond this. The region of Galicia is associated with, among many other things, water and rain, and one of the ongoing interests of developing this project was to express the importance of this element through a "generic roof". In the design, the roof is a sloping convex form, suggesting a large drainpipe. The water it carries runs out through a section of the entrance facade, and collects in a large downpipe, which can easily be identified in an angle of the building.

The light entering at an angle below the roof adds to the overall intention to create a separate, independent building that, through its form, summarizes most of the meaning behind the idea of the prototype. White tiles, beech plywood, painted wood and glass are the basic elements used in the interior spaces, which provide a spacious, light and neutral background to the expressiveness of the roof. The choice of thick, wide ipe wood planks for the facade, contrasting with the zinc plates used for the roof, takes into account the changing tone of the materials - over time, they are expected to take on a velvety gray color, like the old electricity poles scattered through the fields in the area. Finally, the exterior granite base recognizes and pays homage to the material on which it is grounded, the Galician granite ground that this design elevates to the level of an abstract, but real, conditioning.

Three swimming pools have been built using this concept in different contexts within the province of La Coruña. In each case, the design has been adapted to the environment by manipulating the urbanization and the position of some of the openings in the facade, in response to the desire to emphasize particular interior or exterior references. These changes come to identify the specific place in which the building is constructed, without detriment to the expression of the design as a prototype.

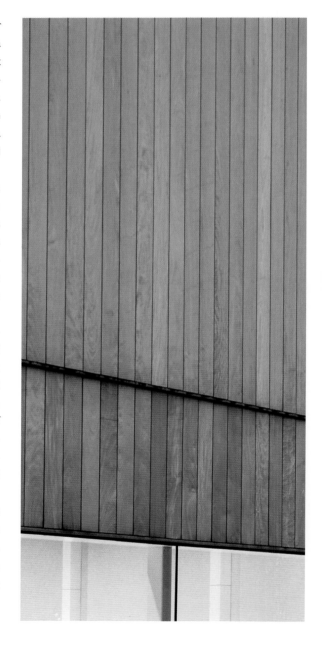

The idea of creating a "prototype" project that could be applied at different sites throughout the region was approached through the idea of a "compact" design. The result is a single volume, in which the longitudinal section reveals the functional layout of the whole.

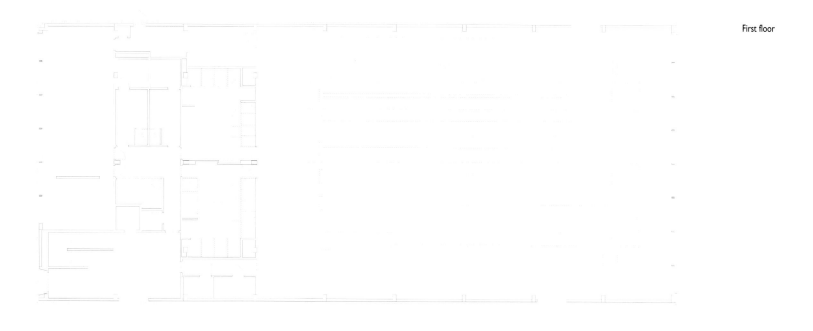

First floor

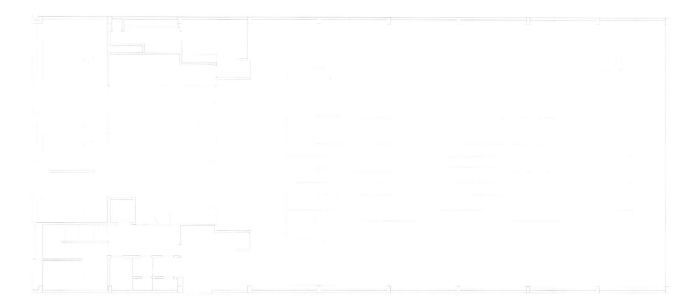

Ground floor

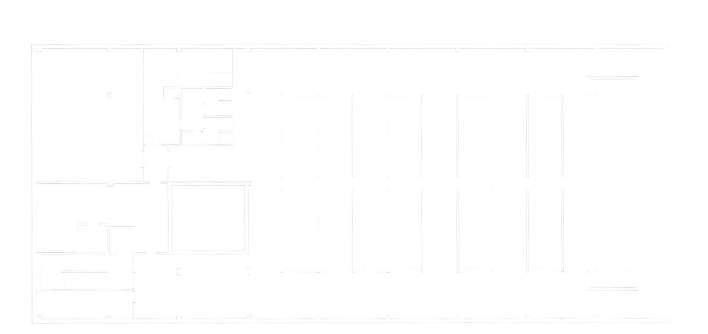

Basement

97

The facade, covered with ipe wood planks, contrasts with the zinc plates used for the roof. Over time, they will acquire a gray velvety tone through the slow, intense process of fusing with the space and landscape that surrounds it.

Elevation A1

Elevation A2

Elevation A3

Elevation A4

The roof is treated as a huge "drainpipe", thus elevating the "rain" that is such an important part of the image of Galicia. In order to emphasize its importance to the design of the project, it takes on a certain independence, which is reflected in the lightweight, laminated wood structure and the glass perimeter of the lateral facades.

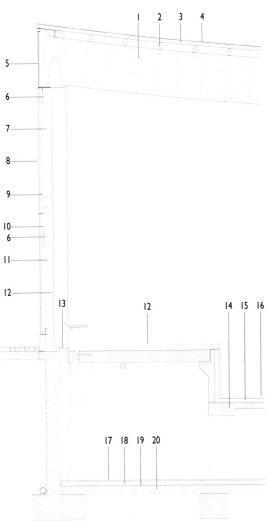
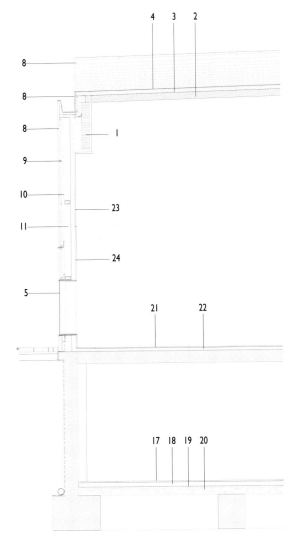

1. 110x18 laminated timber beam
2. 6.5x8 pinewood strips
3. Sandwich panel insulation with acoustic finish, t: 9 cm
4. Zinc over pinewood board
5. 3+3/10/6 Cimalit glass
6. 40x15 concrete strap
7. 50/25 concrete pillar
8. Iroko timber boards, e: 4 cm

9. Projecting insulation
10. Waterproof mortar
11. Block, t: 15 cm
12. 10x10 Non-slip ceramic finish
13. Ventilation grill
14. Reinforced concrete slab, t: 15 cm
15. Sprayed concrete, e: 10 cm
16. 5x5 pool ceramic finish

17. Quartz finish
18. Concrete topping, d: 10 cm
19. Deltadrain-type waterproofing sheet over layer of sand, t: 3cm
20. Gravel
21. Oak timber flooring in gymnasium
22. Silicon sand floor, t: 7cm
23. Painted plaster cladding
24. Beech paneling, t: 2cm

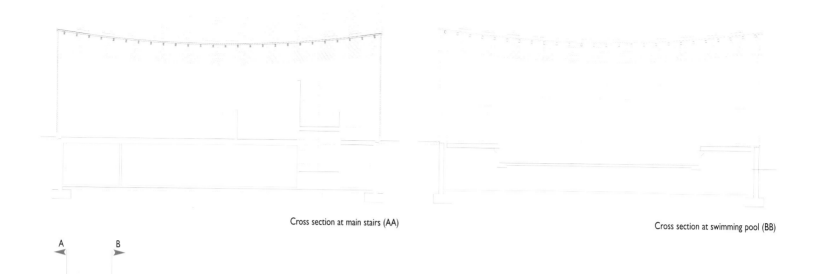

Cross section at main stairs (AA)

Cross section at swimming pool (BB)

A

B

A

B

The pool maintains the principle of maximum transparency, while the dividing centerline takes on a closed character, creating a base for the cafeteria and restaurant, which overlooks the pool area and represents the unity and continuity of the internal space.

Two defining points of the project summarize the identity of the structure, a curved wooden portico that defines the main profile of the building, and the idea of a compact volume that allows the building to adapt to any site, requiring minimal changes.

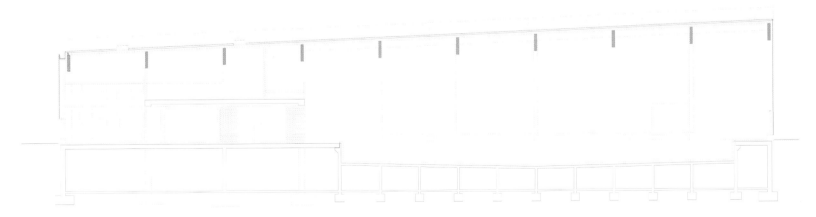

Longitudinal section (CC)

C ▼   ▼ C

The front part of the building contains two large horizontal openings, with the height and position responding to the double attempt to create a direct landscape-like appearance close to the level of the water or the gymnasium.

Rémy Marciano

Ruffi sport complex

Marsella, France

Photographs: Philippe Ruault

The new Ruffi sporting complex was built on the southern part of the site at 96 rue Peyssonnel in the third arrondissement of Marseille, due to future construction plans for the Lajout railway tunnel. It is a place where many different histories intersect and where different scales and housing estates give a sense of pattern and continuity.

Because the project, which consists of a gymnasium and outdoor playing courts, affects the whole city block, the architects considered it essential to organize the empty space, laying out the facilities in relation to the entire site. They placed the new gymnasium opposite the church of St Martín, with the two buildings, face to face, marking out their territory. To emphasize the dialogue between the two buildings, the entry to the sports complex was placed at the axis of the church entrance, and from the lobby and the corridor a break between the changing rooms and the gymnasium frames a view to the neighboring building.

The concrete is like a stone pedestal that emerges from the ground, on which light boxes float. The lighter upper elements rest on the pedestal, defining the gymnasium's presence when night falls. They are placed at the angle required by the slope of the aluminum tray roof.

The disposition of the gymnasium doesn't reach the site limit on the rue Ruffi, allowing playing spaces for pétanque, to be located on the remaining area of sidewalk. A garden completes the setting of the building, maintaining the alignment and allowing the entire the block to be read in a single glance. The gymnasium and its grounds thus provide a meeting point, leisure area, public and playing facilities and a breathing space that revitalizes the neighborhood.

Designed in a period of transformation, the new gymnasium materializes and synthesizes the changes, adopting a critical stance and crystallizing this particular stage of the neighborhood's evolution: the progression from small town, through the industrial era to the contemporary period of re-appropriating the city and its territory.

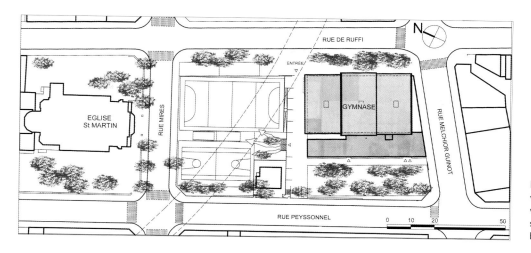

RUE DE RUFFI

N

EGLISE St MARTIN

RUE MIRES

ENTRÉE

GYMNASE

RUE MELCHIOR GUINOT

RUE PEYSSONNEL

0   10   20   50

Like an industrial block, the gymnasium was placed at the angle were rue Ruffi meets rue Melchior Guinot. The concrete, in contact with the street, reveals its outer skin as though it were made of tensed muscles: an opaque pedestal surging from the ground, with light boxes floating above.

0   2   5   10m

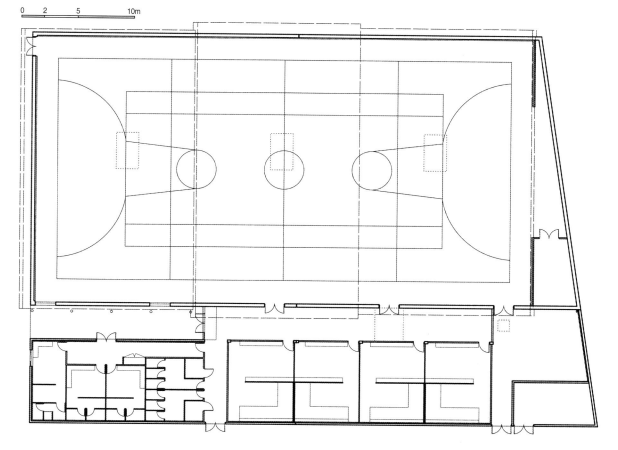

Gymnasium floor plan

107

Longitudinal section

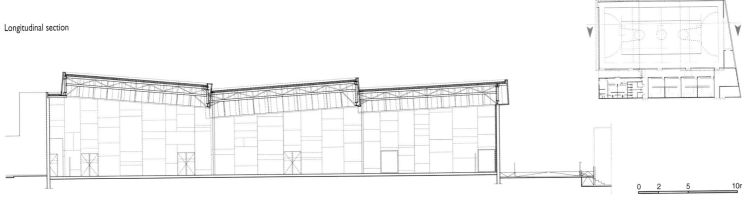

0 2   5   10m

The decision to light and open up the upper areas of the building is not just a response to a particular design concept, but also to the ideal layout for practicing sports: the solid lower sections provide greater resistance to the impact of balls, and provides a better barrier separating the players from the outside world.

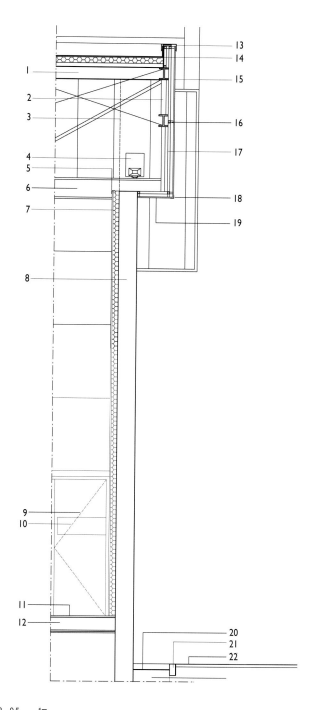

0   0,2   0,5   1m

1. HEB 240 beam
2. Tension beam
3. Ball protection
4. Projector + color filter
5. Galvanized cornice
6. HEB 360 beam
7. Galvanized solid and perforated metallic with riveted over secondary frame + mineral wool
8. 30 cm self-sustaining wall
9. Galvanized metal wall
10. Ceiling
11. TARAFLEX sports flooring over insulating SPORISOL layer

12. Concrete slab
13. Aluminum trim
14. Sealing surface with inbuilt protection over perforated steel tray
15. Danpalon 16 mm polycarbonate coating
16. Aluminum connector
17. Secondary metallic frame
18. Aluminum parapet
19. Lower face, polycarbonate coating
20. Bamboo planting box Leveled edge
21. Variable height pavement
22. Top soil

Thierry Bruttin

Equestrian Center

Granges, Switzerland

Photographs: Contributed by the architect

This project is located on 9 hectares of agricultural land halfway between Sierre and Sion in the heart of Central Valais, a large triangular area with the wooded Rhone dyke as its northern limit and the Rèche irrigation channel to the south. The site opens up naturally towards the east and boasts spectacular views to the Réchy Valley and Central Valais, with the ragged peaks of the Bietschhorn in the distance.

The architect was given the extremely short time of 6 months to build an equestrian center, with the brief including a riding school and stables for the school's own horses, with capacity for 60 horses and sheltered working spaces, a 20 x 60 m pavilion, a jumping and dressage paddock, and all related services and grounds. It also required a canteen with a capacity of 60 to be built as a socializing area for club members and riding school students. And all of this with a limited fixed budget of 2,500,000 francs.

The New School was to be located in a space that was already structured but not yet planned. The stables were placed parallel to the river, a few steps a way from the wooded strip of the Rhone dike, with the planning logic creating two different spaces for teaching and working with horses.

On the right-hand margin, near the entrance, the sheltered working space (pavilion) is located on the west, and the open working space (the paddock) to the east. The two spaces are connected by the "house for the horses", which is like a large, light-filled street where jockeys and students can meet.

Outside, the grounds are on the left-hand margin, with a special area set slightly apart and protected by hedges to allow for the concentration required by this discipline: the dressage test.

The bar, placed in the middle and slightly raised, offers extensive views over the pavilion, where the outdoor jumping practice takes place.

In terms of construction, the time available and the size of the project made it necessary to use prefabricated elements, with appropriate materials chosen for the different parts. Wood was used to build the pavilion and canteen, while the stables are made of reinforced concrete.

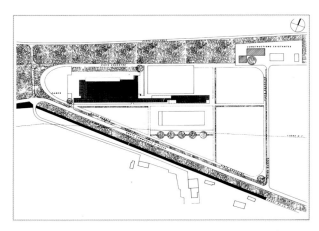

The 9 hectare site occupied by the equestrian center has a special and privileged position in relation to the Réchy Valley, the Central Valais and, in the distance, the rugged peaks of the Bietschhorn.

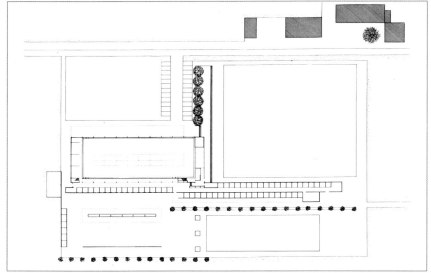

Among other services, the center includes a riding school, stables for 60 horses, indoor working areas, a 20mx60m pavilion, a paddock for jumping and dressage, and all related grounds and services.

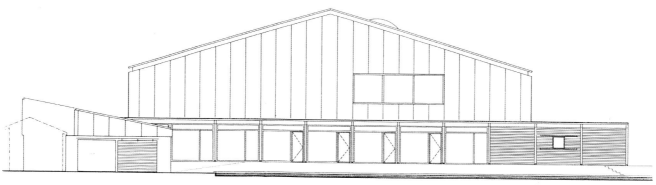

Front elevation of the pavilion from the paddock.

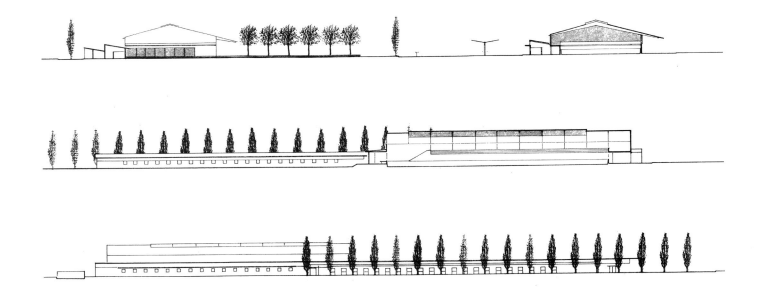

Side and front elevations of the equestrian center complex.

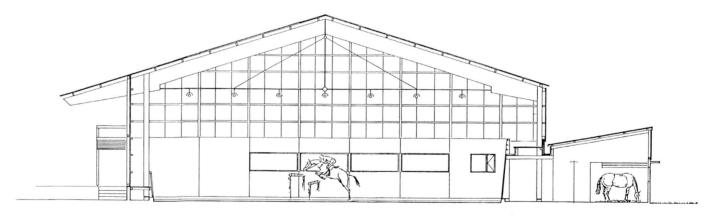

Cross section, pavilion.

Detlef Sacker

Multi-use pavilion
in the Erich-Kästner-Schule

Donaueschingen, Germany

Photographs: Roland Halbe / ARTUR

The new multi-use pavilion, together with the existing Erich-Kästner school, creates a U-shaped complex that is open at the side facing the center of the school. In future, this clearly defined urban space can be used as a sheltered playground area. The street access to the pavilion is clearly marked by a distinctive entrance.

The main body of the pavilion is separated from the lobby and the adjacent building by continuous glazing. This, together with the glazing of the pavilion to the north, near the green zone, provides high-quality natural lighting to the interior space. The building's spaciousness is emphasized even further by the glazing of the outer wall of the two-story foyer and the visitors' gallery on the top floor, with views to the pavilion.

The natural coloring of the materials used has mostly been left untouched, and the warmth of the wood contrasts with the raw concrete and anthracite-colored metal sections. A system of natural ventilation and nocturnal air-conditioning ensure that the air is high-quality at low cost for all kinds of activities and sporting events. The foyer is screened from sunlight by panels of photovoltaic modules.

www.sacker.de

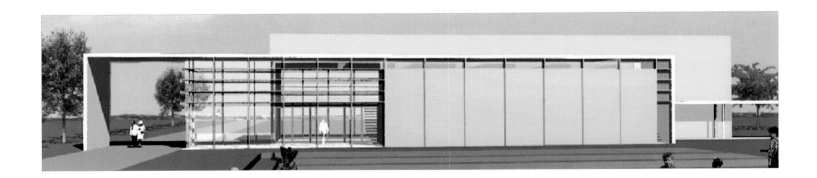

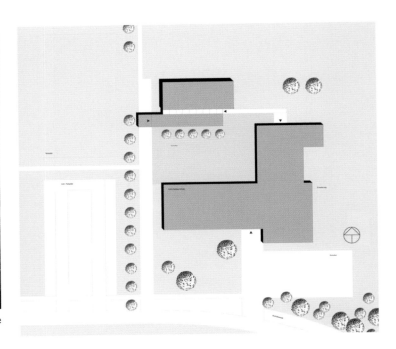

This multifunctional pavilion, together with the existing Erich-Kästner school, defines a space can in future be used as a covered playground.

1. Foyer
2. Multi-use sports area
3. Kitchen
4. Adapted locker room
5. Sports equipment room
6. Technical rooms
7. Storage area
8. Internal communication center
   locker room - sports area

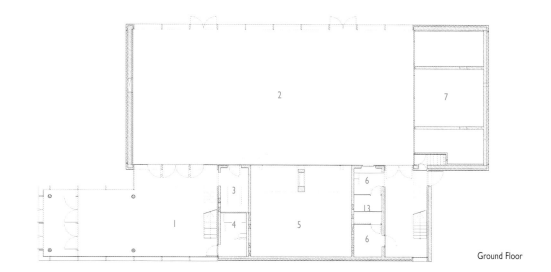

Ground Floor

1. Foyer
2. Multi-use sports area
3. Service platform
4. Girls WC
5. Girls locker room
6. Girls showers
7. Staff bathrooms
8. Girls WC
9. Boys locker room
10. Boys showers
11. Internal communication center
    locker room - sports area
12. Gallery

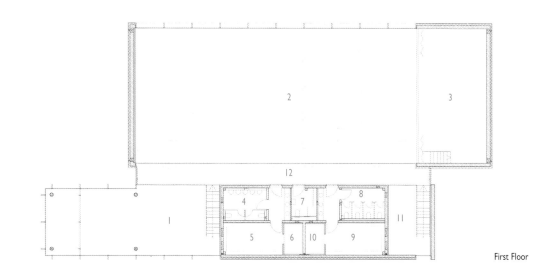

First Floor

The court area, and the platform raised at one end, emphasizes the multi-use nature of the main enclosure.

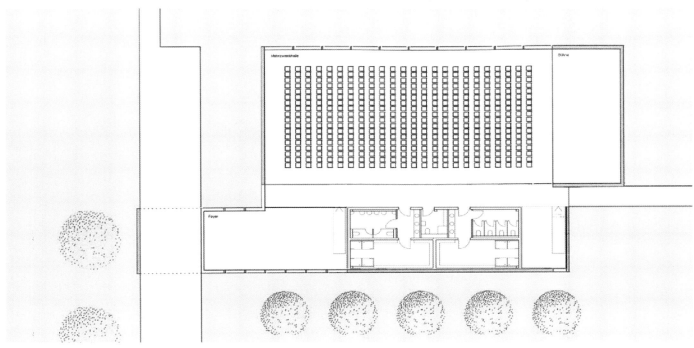

123

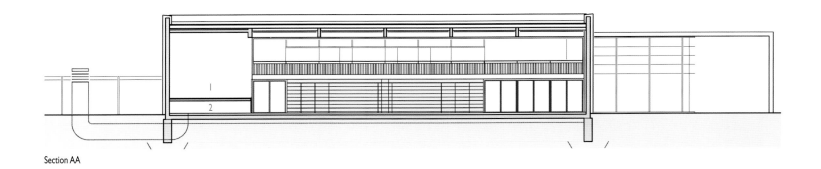

Section AA

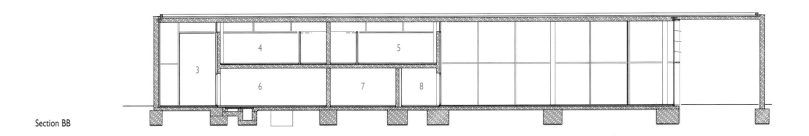

Section BB

1. Service platform
2. Storage area
3. Internal communication center
   locker room - sports area
4. Girls locker room
5. Boys locker room
6. Technical room
7. Sports equipment room
8. Kitchen
9. Multi-use sports area
10. Gallery

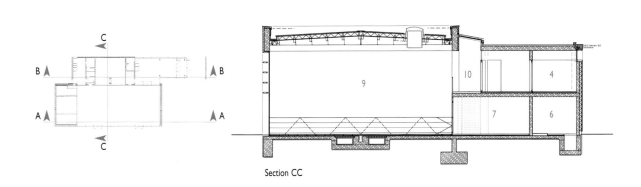

Section CC

North elevation

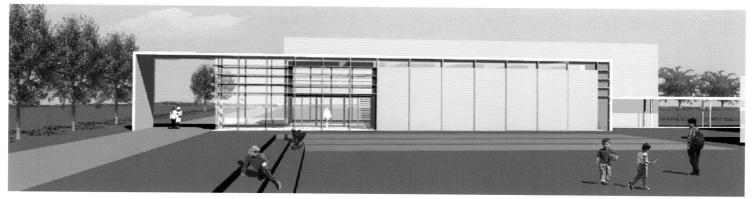

South elevation

The building's size is emphasized by the external glazing of the double-story lobby and the visitors' gallery on the upper floor, with views to the pavilion.

Nicolas Michelin

Gymnasium Europole

Grenoble, France

Photographs: Hervé Abbadie

The brief for this project required a gymnasium of the same dimensions as the site, and so the building occupies the entire site. It consists of a concrete base supporting a steel structure, which is covered with a polycarbonate membrane that serves as both roof and façade. The ground floor is made from three parallel concrete walls that define the dressing rooms and bathrooms, and support the concrete slabs of the sports hall. To the east, an additional 24 x 14 m room is built as a continuation of the dressing rooms.

Blue polycarbonate was chosen because of its ability to regulate the interior temperature. A system of revolving panels ensures natural ventilation for the sports hall. Eight specially created loudspeakers, suspended from the ceiling like oversized lamps, serve to correct the acoustics of the large space, and integrate the lighting equipment.

As specified in the original brief, the gymnasium occupies the entire site, sitting like a huge awning inserted into the urban environment.

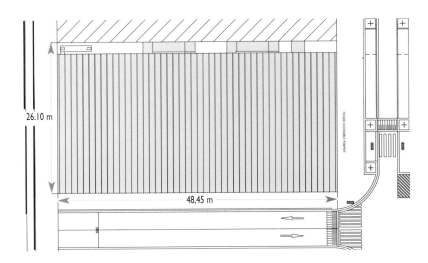

26.10 m

48,45 m

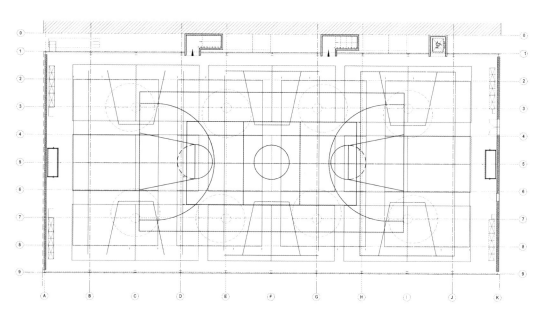

Floor plan

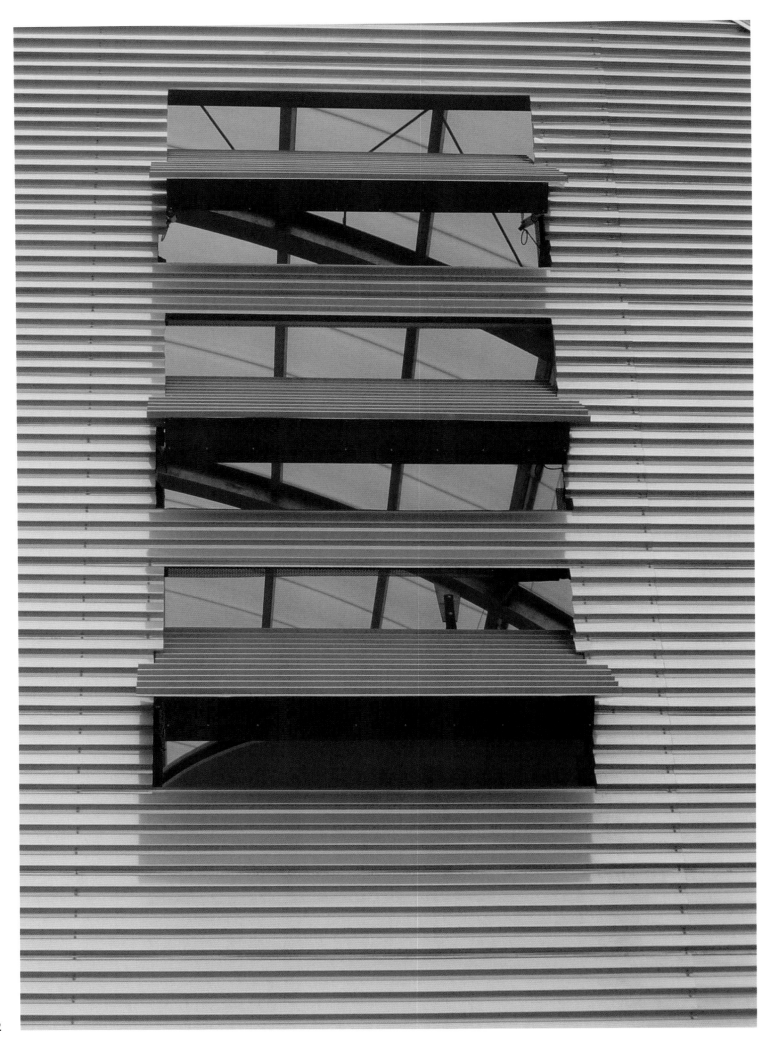

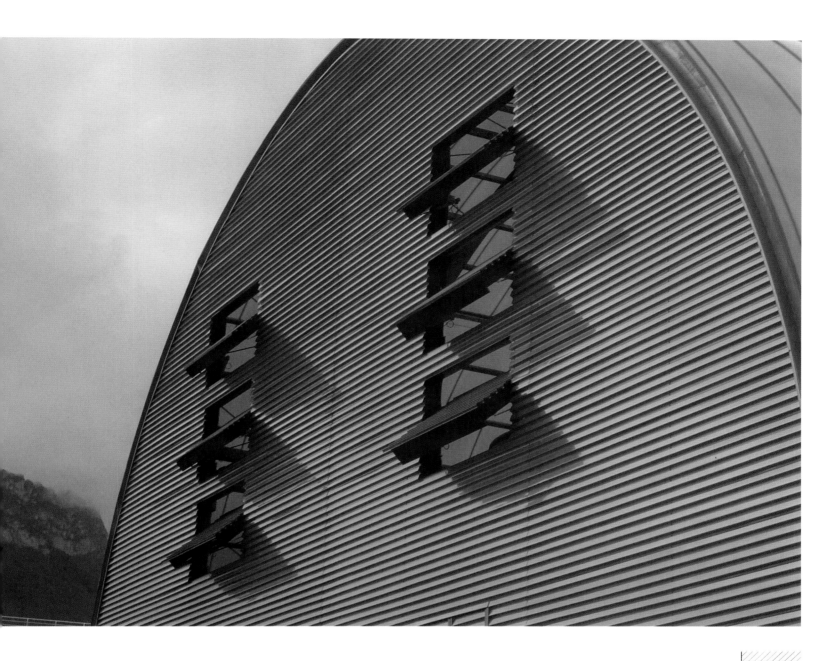

The concrete base supports a steel structure covered by a polycarbonate skin that serves as both façade and roof. On the lower floor, where the changing rooms and showers are located, three parallel concrete walls support the concrete floor of the sports hall.

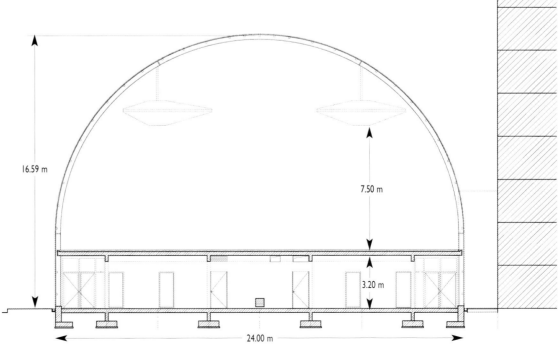

16.59 m

7.50 m

3.20 m

24.00 m

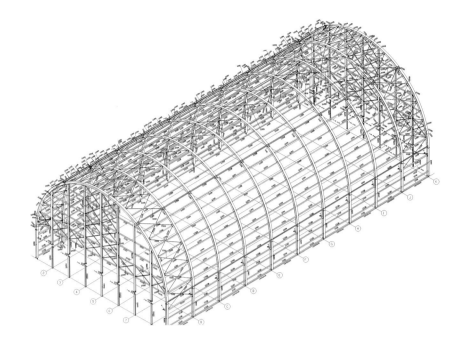

The polycarbonate used to cover the external facade of the building emphasizes the atmosphere of lightness, and its blue color changes in response to the light.

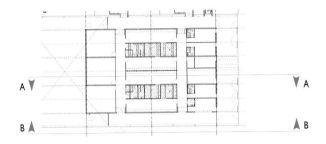

Section AA

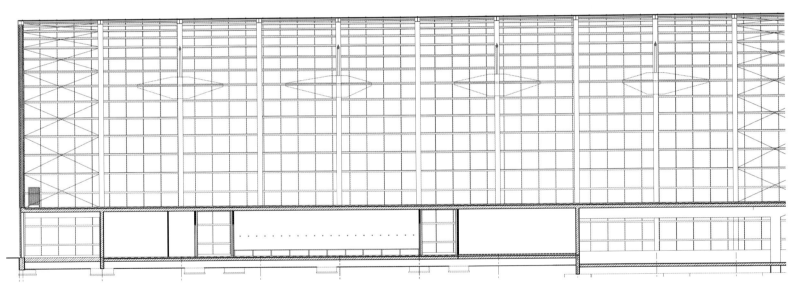

Section BB

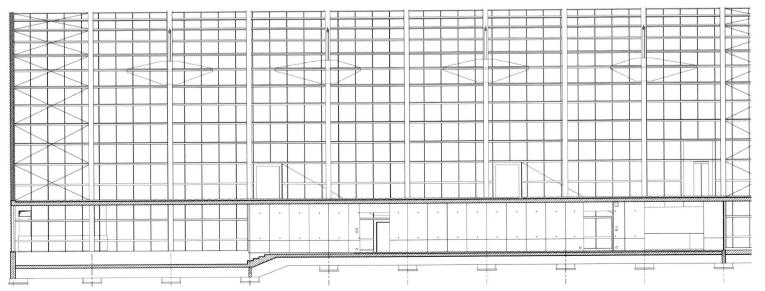

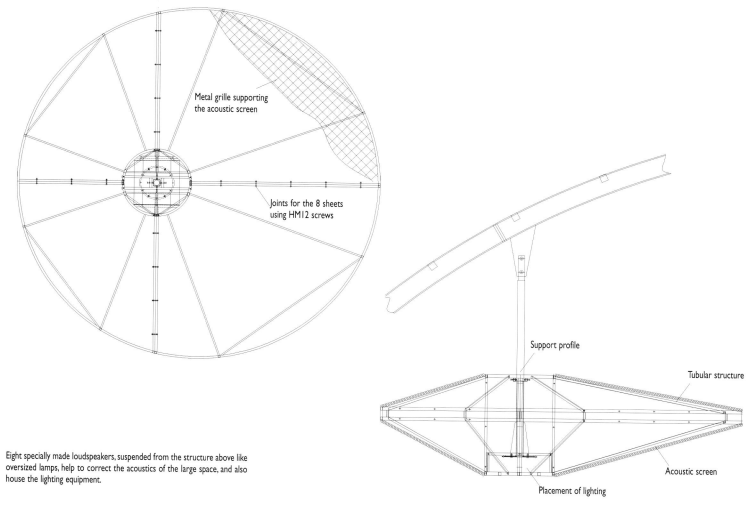

Metal grille supporting
the acoustic screen

Joints for the 8 sheets
using HM12 screws

Support profile

Tubular structure

Acoustic screen

Placement of lighting

Eight specially made loudspeakers, suspended from the structure above like oversized lamps, help to correct the acoustics of the large space, and also house the lighting equipment.

Mario Corea Aiello + Francisco Gallardo

Swimming Pool in Vilafranca

Vilafranca del Penedès, Spain

Photographs: Jordi Miralles

The location of this building had two fundamental purposes: to make a decisive contribution to the urban planning of the sporting area, and to make the most efficient use of the material resources of some of the existing installations. The project consolidates the previously built swimming pools, creating an aquatic center that gives a clear sense of continuity in relation to the buildings and management, while also increasing the potential for different kinds of water sports.

The limits on the stages of construction were fundamental in the planning of this project. For this reason, the building was planned as three large areas that could almost be built in an autonomous way and independently of each other, with the shared entry module complementing all of them.

The materials used respond to the need to satisfy the functional, aesthetic and energy saving criteria required by public installations. The project had to allow easy maintenance, both intrinsically and in regards to the configuration and placement in the works, which had to be largely visible and / or able to be documented. The structure was made of reinforced concrete, with the exception of the roof girders of the pool areas, which are made of glued laminated wood. The curved roof is a "sandwich" construction, with an internal tongued and grooved timber sheet, glass fiber thermal insulation and an exterior lacquered aluminum layer.

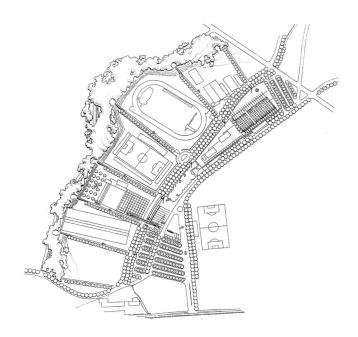

The project aimed to consolidate the existing swimming pools and complement them with new aquatic installations for various uses.

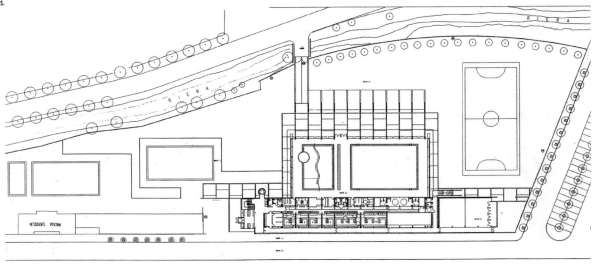

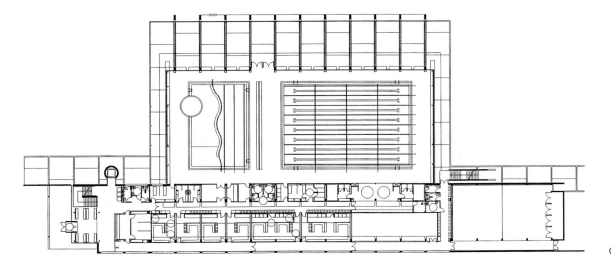

Ground Floor

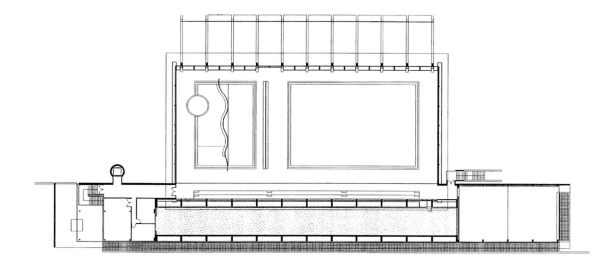

First Floor

The internal structure of wooden girders is reflected on the outside with a similar system of reinforced concrete girders.

The elegance of the curve that resolves the geometry of the roof is clearly
visible from this aerial perspective of the complex.

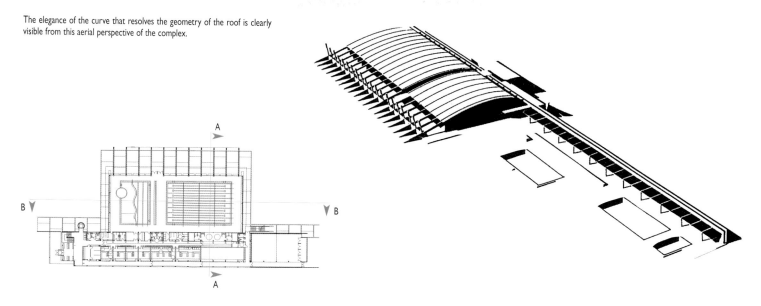

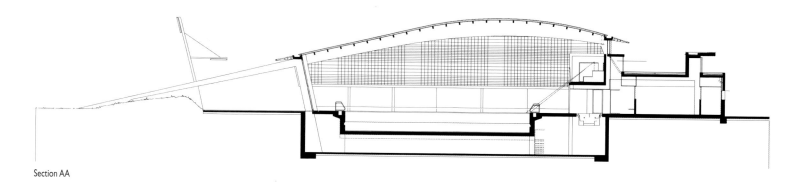

Section AA

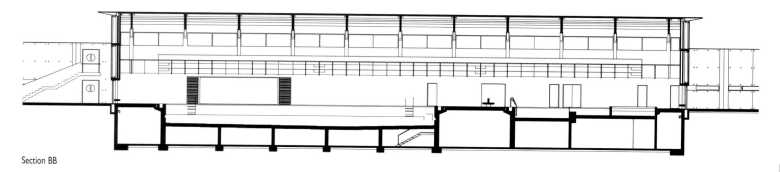

Section BB

The roof of the pool, supported by glued laminated wood, is a "sandwich" construction made from tongue and grooved timber, glass fiber insulation and a lacquered aluminum sheet.

Aranda Pigem Vilalta Arquitectes

Athletics Stadium Tussols-Basil

Girona, Spain

Photographs: Eugeni Pons

This athletics stadium, located in natural surroundings, emphasizes the existing natural features and brings track and field events back to nature. The track is set in a clearing in an oak forest, where an interplay is set up between the degrees of relationship between the track and the forest areas: the adjacent forest, the forest beyond, and the forest in the distance, with the grandstands forming small slopes or terraces between clearings.

In the initial stages, the large size of the track made its placement difficult. The architects decided creatively re-imagine the way a track works, placing man, running, back in nature.

The project evolved in the midst of confrontations between athletes and ecologists: the former didn't want there to be any trees, the latter were against the trees being felled. In the end, the clearing in the oak forest, which had previously been cultivated fields, was transformed into a positive space that continued on beyond its limits, and some of the rare, slowly-maturing, hundred-year old oak trees were conserved in the interior of the track area

The stadium itself is set deeply onto the surrounding terrain, and the grandstands were built to create small slopes on either side. The architects were able to show that it is not impossible to comply with the strict federal regulations on visibility of the tracks for the judges while conserving nature... and as in the ancient Greek games, they rediscovered the Mediterranean esplanade created from a clearing in the woods.

This athletics stadium, with its track carved delicately into the topography of the site is an example of wise and innovative interpretation of landscape.

The terrace and small slopes contribute to the topographical adaptation, and act as grandstands for the public.

The towers emerging from the dense tree trunks create a dialogue and establish references in the space, while the trees in the intermediate area act as filters that change according to the seasons.

153

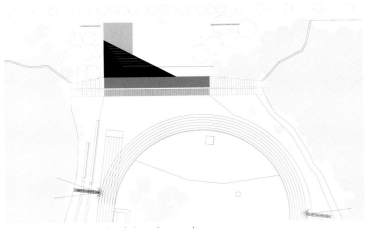

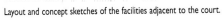
Layout and concept sketches of the facilities adjacent to the court.

© RCR

Model of the volume and longitudinal and cross sections.

1

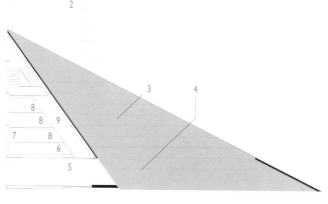

2

10 ——————   9   —————— 10

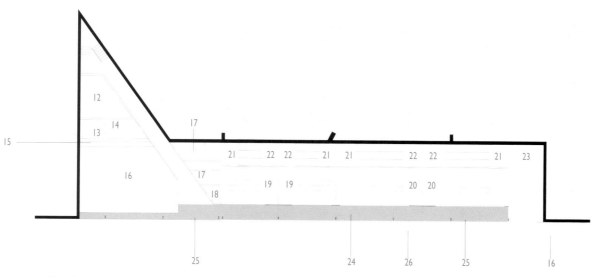

1. Bicycle lane	10. Access ramp to grandstand and locker rooms	19. Group locker rooms
2. Access ramp	11. Access ramp to locker rooms and soccer field	20. Shared locker room
3. Pacilities entrance verandah	12. Technical equipment room	21. Bathrooms for disabled access
4. Entrance	13. Bathrooms and locker rooms for disabled access	22. Showers for disabled access
5. Bar	14. Infirmary	23. Court equipment storage
6. Bar-control	15. Equipment locker	24. Meeting area
7. Storage	16. Bodybuilding room	25. Court exit
8. Bathrooms	17. Technician-referees locker rooms	26. Outside terrace
9. Terrace - lookout	18. Storage	

Javier Pérez Urribarri. Estudio ACXT, Grupo IDOM

Indoor pool in the Colegio Vizcaya

Zamudio, Spain

Photographs: César San Millán

The design for this project is the result of a restricted competition organized by the Colegio Vizcaya. It consists of a building containing an indoor swimming pool, dressing rooms, a landscaped space for an indoor kindergarten, storage areas and spaces for services and facilities.

The proposed design was dome-shaped and used mainly prefabricated, tunnel-like concrete materials, with the external walls and ceiling built at the same time. This system allowed the main part of the structure, the domes, to be built in two weeks, thus decreasing the risk of accidents to students and the effect of the construction work on the school's teaching activities, which it was important not to interrupt.

The vaulted form was designed in response to three objectives, insulation, quick construction and suitability for a covered garden for children's activities; a fourth, perhaps more poetic reason, is the reference to a cave as a secret place, a space that appears in the imaginary world of so many children's and young adult's books.

The use of the prefabricated concrete elements and the false-tunnel technique allowed the architects to place a garden on the upper part of the building. The contour of the dome minimizes the risk of water leakage, compared to a flat design, as the water that filters through the soil travels down the curved surface to the drains placed longitudinally at the base. The way the project was executed meant that the children's pay area could remain at the level of the courtyard and conserve it's "green" character.

The design of a semi-underground, dome-shaped building with a layer of soil ranging from one to four meters above each parameter, gives the design unbeatable insulation and a stable indoor temperature throughout the year (the cellar effect), eliminating thermal peaks and leading to a notable decrease in energy consumption. The materials used are easy to maintain, durable and attractive.

From the outside, the building has a minimal visual impact. It seems to be a new hill, a new elevation in the landscape. From the side that slopes towards the soccer field, two eyes, the swimming pool and the dressing room, are the only signs that there is a building below the line of the hill.

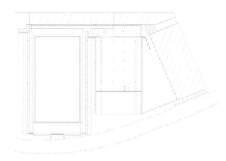

The proposed solution organized the built space into two zones defined by two large domes, which have been integrated into the landscap e like two artificial hills. These prefabricated concrete "cut and cover" domes have enabled gardened spaces to be included in the upper portion.

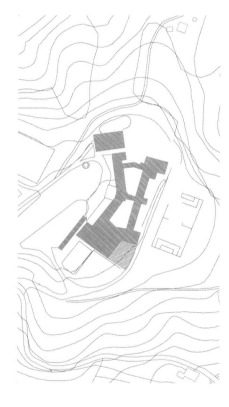

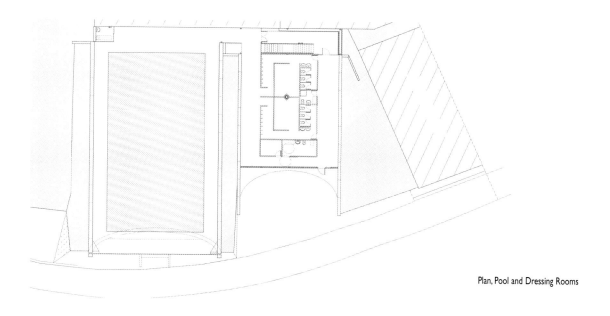

Plan, Pool and Dressing Rooms

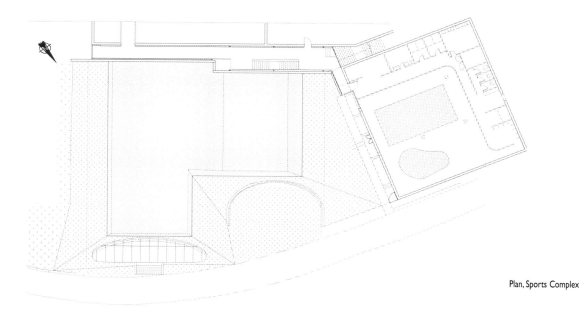

Plan, Sports Complex

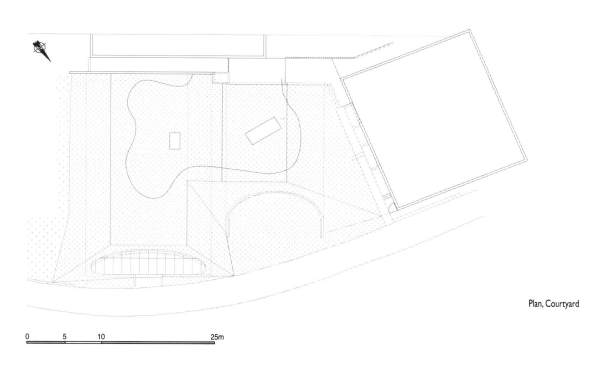

Plan, Courtyard

0   5   10   25m

A large dome, 5.5 meters at its highest point, covers the pool, and the glass facade provides extensive views towards Derio, Sondika and Zamudio. A smaller dome, divided horizontally, houses the dressing rooms, with rooms for installations on the lower floor. The two domes are joined by a corridor near the sports complex, which can be used to access the pool area and also connects the existing buildings and provides an extra external exit to the soccer field.

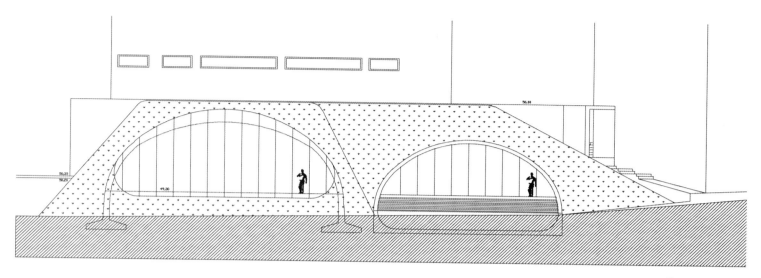

Elevation to soccer field

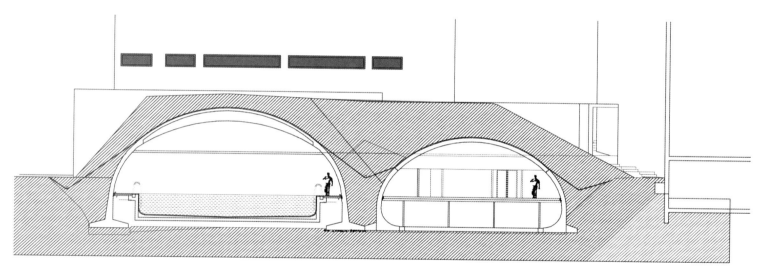

Cross section swiming pool

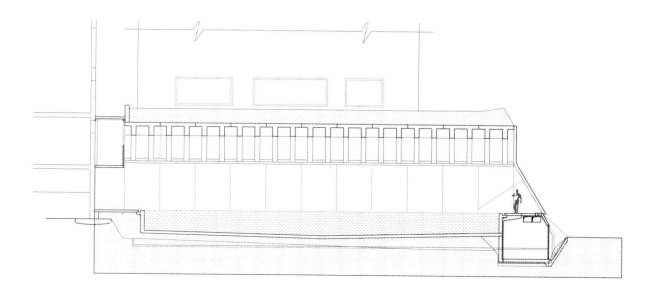

Longitudinal section swiming pool

0   2   5   10m

In the dressing rooms, the wet areas have been completely separated from the dry areas. The showers are wide corridors that have to be passed through (like a shower tunnel) on the way to and from the pool. The whole lower part of the dressing room dome is set aside for services and facilities.

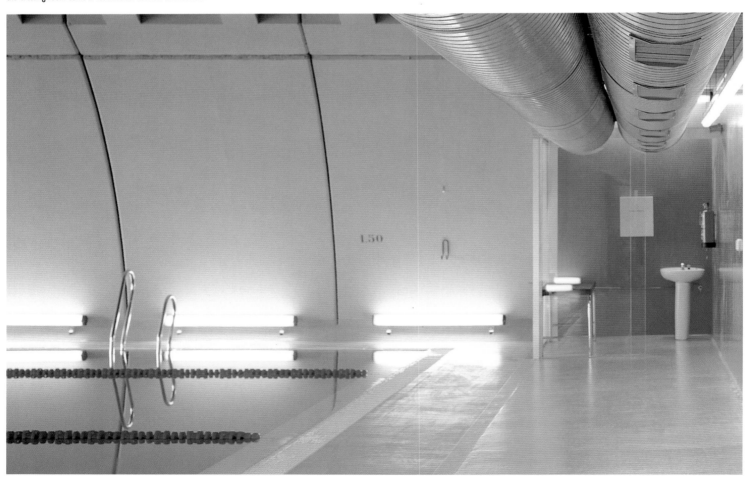

Kisho Kurokawa Architect and Associates

Fujinomiya Golf Club Clubhouse

Shizuoka, Japan

Photographs: Tomio Ohashi

Fujinomiya Golf Club had a reputation as one of the most prestigious golf courses, and for a long time it was well-loved not only by club members but also many other golfers. Due to the aging of the clubhouse, a reconstruction plan including extra land for patting practice had been developed.

The club is situated on a rise in the western part of Nishinomiya city, which is recognized as a first-class scenic district for its deep green characteristics. The reconstruction plan was developed within strict regulations such as an 8m maximum height and high ratio of green areas.

The clubhouse is a reinforced concrete structure consisting of 2 stories and a basement. The entrance hall is a single-story space, and other parts like the locker rooms and restaurant are built one over the other vertically, creating double-story areas.

The configuration of the building is expressed as two volumes, composed of flat surfaces connected by expansion joints. An egg-shaped core is located at the center of each volume, with a number of randomly spaced columns surrounding them. Visitors can come and go freely between these columns. The exterior wall of the building is made from exposed concrete glass and aluminum. The canopy is fixed to the ground, and a number of flat aluminum bars are embedded under it.

The visitor area is surrounded by clear glass, and the exterior and interior of the building flow into each other. By slanting the wall surface the façade 8 degrees, the direct sunlight into the building is minimized and at the same time the reflection of the glass façade on the exterior is effectively reduced. The outline of the building is composed of the curved lines of fractal geometry. The view of Mt Fuji from the building was carefully taken into account in the design. Not just from the rooftop, but also from the restaurant, the bathrooms and the entrance hall, the whole figure of Mt Fuji bursts in to the building through its openings.

The club is embedded into an exceptional landscape, high on a hill on the western side of the city of Nishinomiya, with views to Mt Fuji. The project involved reconstructing the old golf club and creating a space for putting practice.

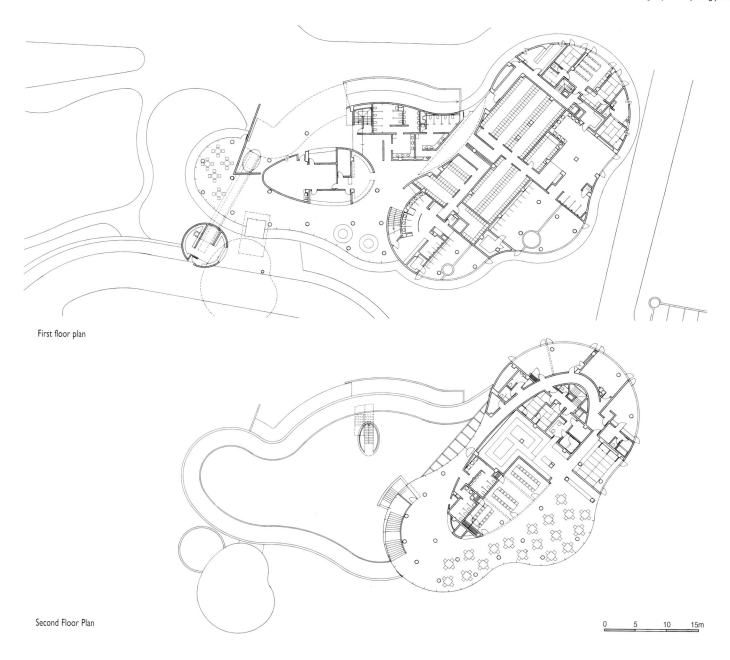

First floor plan

Second Floor Plan

0   5   10   15m

The shape of the building is based on the curves of fractal geometry, and the glass façade slopes in order to minimize reflections outside and avoid sunlight glare inside.

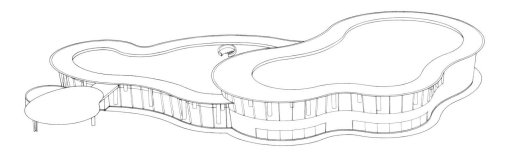

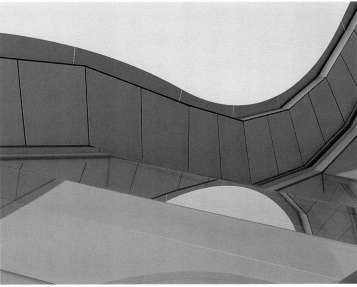

The imposing figure of Mt Muji bursts in through the glass surfaces, an image that adds incomparable value to the building's interior.

one room huber/meinhart + walter schuster

Police Sports Club Salzburg

Salzburg, Austria

Photographs: Andrew Phelps

The brief for this project was to design a clubhouse alongside existing playing fields for the largest local sports association in Salzburg. The requirements were a 30 m x 16 m hall to accommodate judo, taekwondo and other sports, as well as dressing rooms and locker areas.

The site presented particular characteristics, being the interface between the commercial strip to the south of the town (with large container buildings) and an extensive, protected parkland area stretching between Freisaal and Hellbrunn castles.

On the northern side of the fields, a busy avenue links the "alpenstrasse" car and shopping area with the tranquil green space.

The project was selected through a limited architectural competition, and places the building near the residential buildings at the site's northern end. With the trees and tall neighboring buildings, directly across from the start of the avenue, the building gives the impression of a gateway. The main volume is pillared, drawing special attention to the location and opening a dialogue with the surrounding buildings. On the other hand, the open ground floor emphasizes the flow of movement into the green area, and creates a feeling of transparency, ease and continuity. The "free" form is a sign of the building's purpose as a sports hall, and also a link with nature.

The building consists of a steel skeleton "shelved" with concrete floors and anchored to a concrete core. The unusually shaped structure, together with wood and glass elements, are enveloped n a silvery, holohedral sheet skin, studded with horizontal rows of windows to provide natural light to the interior.

The project, which was commissioned through a restricted design competition, involved designing a club for a sports association. The building's facilities include a 16 x 30 m room for judo, taekwondo and other sports, as well as changing rooms and lockers.

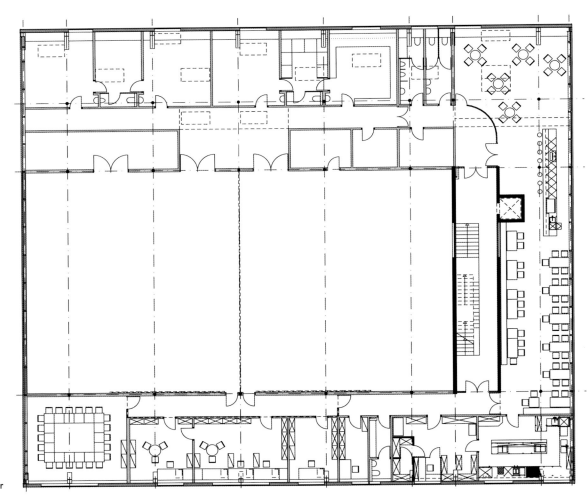

First Floor

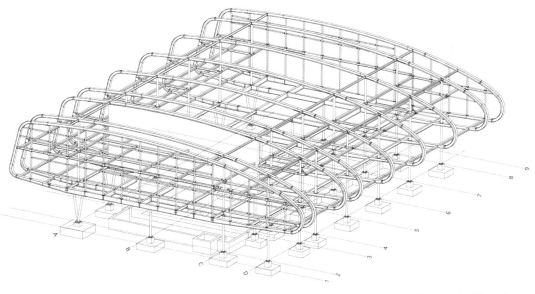

Axonometric of the steel structure. The use of steel, which seems to be in its raw state without any finish in some spaces, creates an industrial feel in both the interior and exterior of the building.

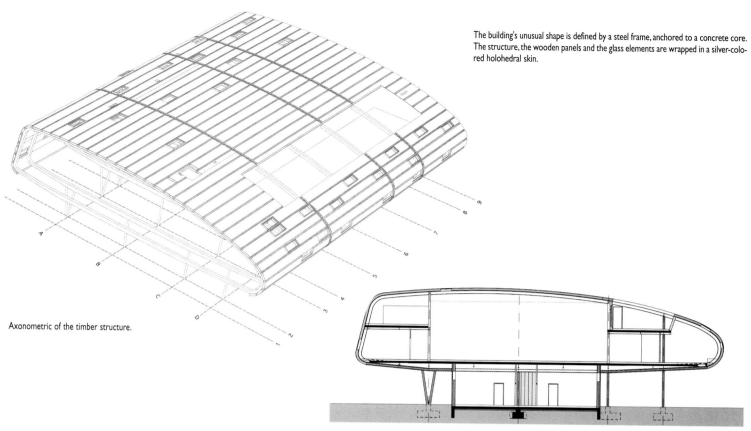

The building's unusual shape is defined by a steel frame, anchored to a concrete core. The structure, the wooden panels and the glass elements are wrapped in a silver-colored holohedral skin.

Axonometric of the timber structure.

Cross section

MAP Arquitectes

Municipal Indoor Swimming Pool in Can Gibert del Pla

Girona, Spain

Photographs: Duccio Malagamba

This municipal indoor swimming pool is located in an area of urban expansion, on a site that is partially occupied by a Primary Health Care Center, the old Santa Eugènia cemetery and a small green zone in front of the old High School, including all the pedestrian circulation to and from the school. The architects took these urban, circulation and orientation factors as a starting point to resolve the new building in relationship to the existing facilities.

The technical specifications of the regional government's sports authority's recommendations are very precise for this kind of project, specifying a single, compact building with south-facing glass wall for the swimming pool area. This particular pavilion is composed of two volumes forming an L-shaped building. The first volume contains the swimming pool and spectator area, while the second contains the additional areas and a gym with body building equipment. The layout of the building creates an inner courtyard in the middle of the block. The space occupied by the adjacent cemetery is formally incorporated into the configuration of the new design, an archaic preexisting element within a new space, similar in scale to the new intervention.

In the exterior spaces a distinction is made between the private and public areas. The courtyard is closed off on the side of the busiest road and treated as a garden. The design incorporates the cemetery wall and adds landscaping, taking into account the view from the swimming pool. The spaces adjacent to the Health Care Center are oriented towards more public and intense use, in keeping with pedestrian access to the High School. Finally, in the area leading to the building, a large overhang indicates the entrance to users of the center.

The volume containing the dressing rooms and showers has been constructed from reinforced concrete: pillars, edge girders and walls were built "in situ"; the floor and ceiling are made of hollow core prestressed concrete slabs and the facade is made from reinforced concrete lined with CFC-free polyester foam on the interior, and water-repellant DM boards. The outer wall also has an anti-graffiti treatment. This section has an inverted type roof.

In the pool section, finishes were applied to all the concrete surfaces in order to prevent them reacting with the chlorine, and the girders were protected with a layer of anodized aluminum. The facade is built as a "sandwich" of prefabricated reinforced concrete elements, thick enough to avoid condensation forming. For this section, the architects chose to use a conventional roof.

In accordance with the rules of the original competition, the project takes into account the maintenance conditions and eco-energy efficiency of the new swimming pool facilities.

The floor plan of the building is L-shaped, with the swimming pool and spectator areas in one wing, and the additional spaces and gym equipment room in the other. A large overhang indicates the entrance to users of the center.

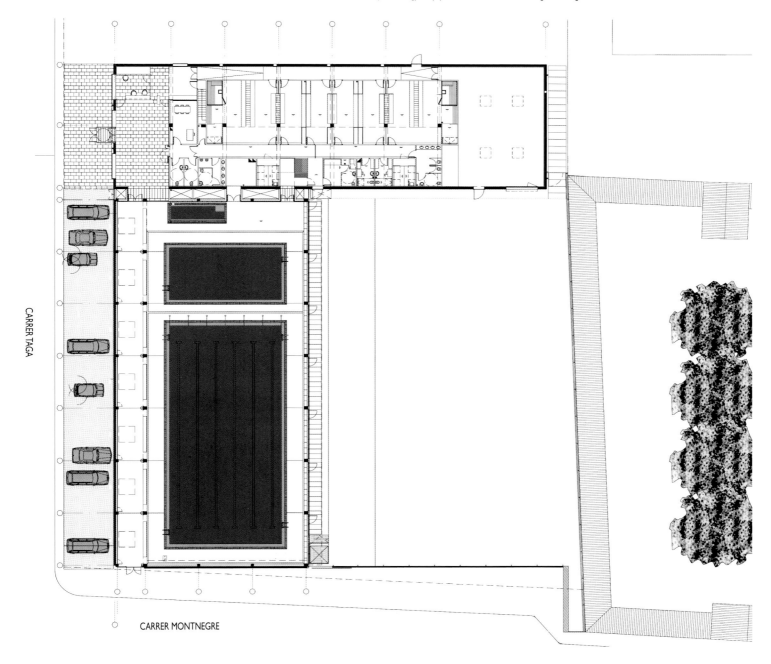

CARRER TAGA

CARRER MONTNEGRE

There some fixed and some movable parts that allow access from the pool to the landscaped rear area, and can also provide ventilation for the pool area in summer.

As far as possible, the building methods and materials used have been local, durable, with a low environmental impact and the ability to resist the aggressions of the internal and external environments.

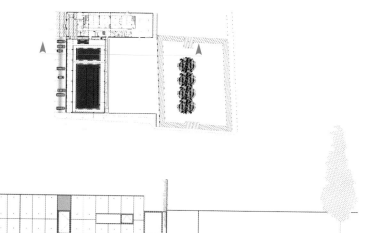

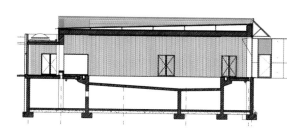

gmp - von Gerkan, Marg und Partner - Architects
design: Meinhard von Gerkan

Private tennis court in Jurmala

Riga, Latvia

Photographs: Klaus Frahm

Jurmala is a seaside resort of Riga, the Latvian capital. At a distance of approximately 20 km from the city center, the town stretches along the Baltic Sea in a coastal strip wooded with pines. A banker family commissioned the GMP (von Gerkan, Marg und Partner Architects) team to plan a comprehensive extension of the Villa Marta including, amongst other things, a guesthouse and an indoor tennis court.

The guesthouse and tennis pavilion are oriented along the strict road grid and frame the old villa. With their restricted eaves height, these new structures integrate seamlessly into the scale of the surrounding country houses.

The pavilion and the other new buildings make reference to the traditional timber construction typical of the area, transferring this construction system into the present. The unusual cable bracings of the load-bearing structure and the mono-pitch roofs of the skylights give the exterior of the building its distinctive appearance.

The roof surfaces of the tennis pavilion are inclined, echoing the sloping nature of the surrounding roofs, and the mono-pitch and hip roofs are clad with sheet zinc.

Like the guesthouse, the tennis pavilion is designed as a timber frame structure, with the façades finished with Siberian larch timber cladding.

The load-bearing structure consists of columns that are re-anchored with stay ropes to the foundation. These cantilever beams support a total of eleven truss girders that span the court, and the shed roof structure allows the north light to enter into the pavilion. The aubergine wall paneling made from coated timber elements defines the interior atmosphere, while the hall's visible frame construction of light larch structures the space. Due to their elevated position a total of 90 seats along the longitudinal sides offer an optimal view onto the sunken court.

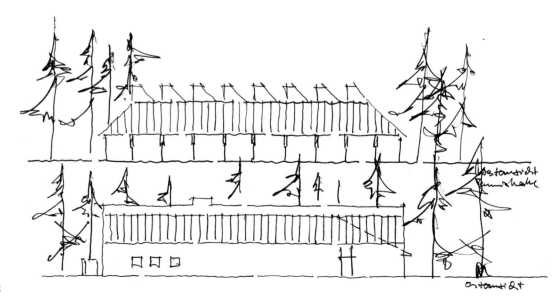

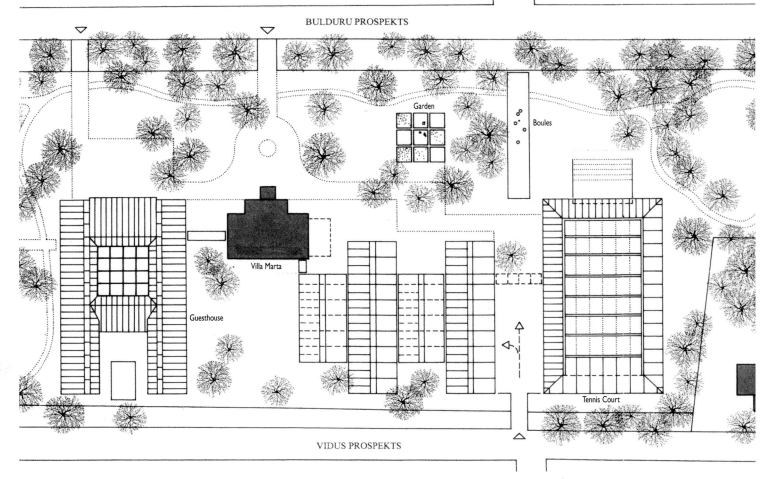

Placement of the tennis court within the Villa Marta residence.

The external shape of the pavilion housing the tennis court, with its eaves mono-pitch roofs and zinc finishes, echoes the traditional local architecture.

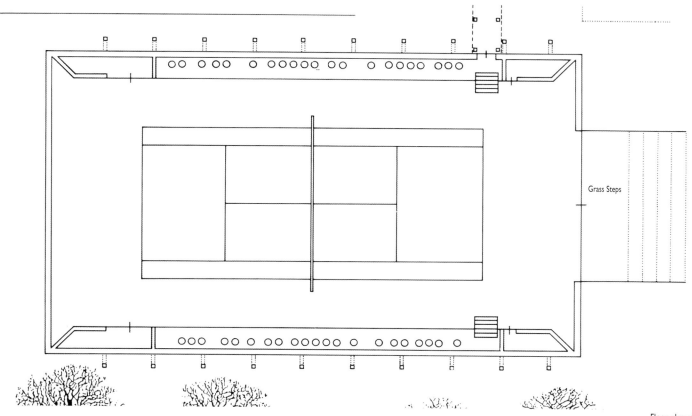

Grass Steps

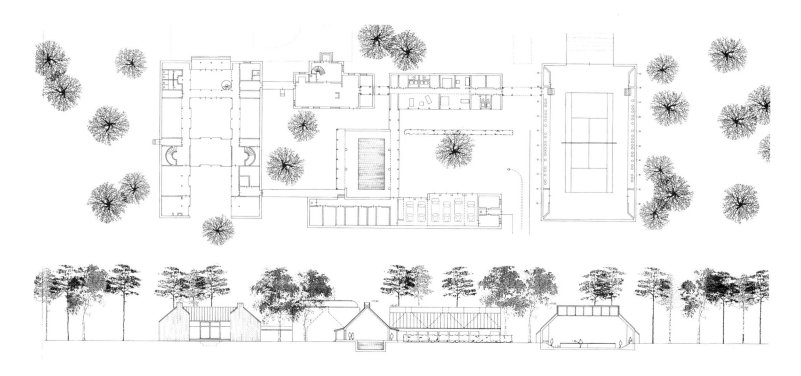

The layout of the external elements of the structure, which is re-anchored with stay ropes to the foundation, is a distinctive feature of the building. The façade has been clad with Siberian larch wood, the same material that was used for the structure of the pavilion.

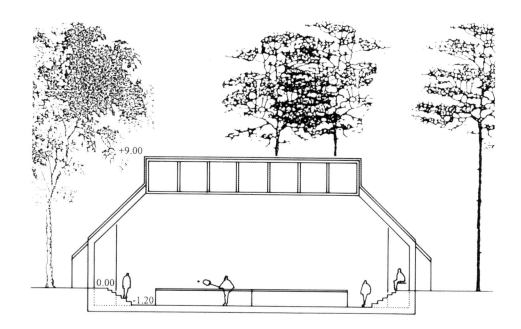

Cross section

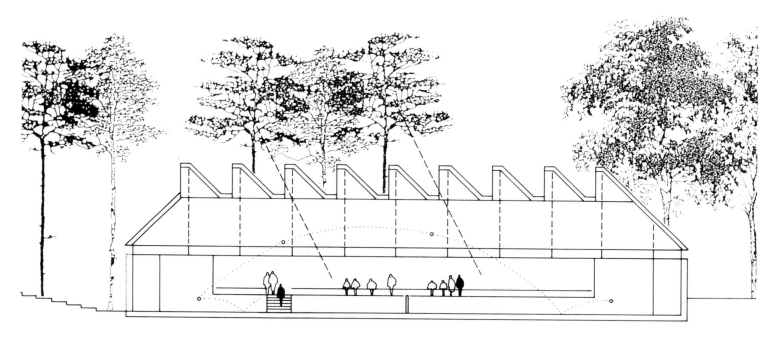

Longitudinal section

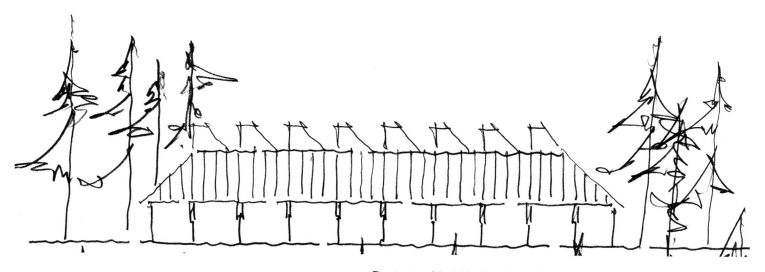

The orientation of the skylights allows the north light to enter through the trusses providing uniform lighting and minimizing glare.

Fink + Jocher

Ballspielhalle Ingosltadt

Ingolstadt, Germany

Photographs: Simone Rosenberg & Fink + Jocher

The sports- hall (30 m x 45 m x 8 m) is used both by the neighbouring High School and of local sportsclub.
The part of the gymnasium oriented to the north was provided as timber construction.
A two-storey building-part in the south, which takes up the different secondary rooms, was build as reinforced concrete construction.
The entire building cover consists of a glassprofile wall-system, which is filled with translucent thermal insulation between the two glass profile bowls. The two rows of large format aluminium windowelements within the upper and lower range of the north fassade as well as in the servicepart in the south of the building, protects the sportshall against excessive overheating.

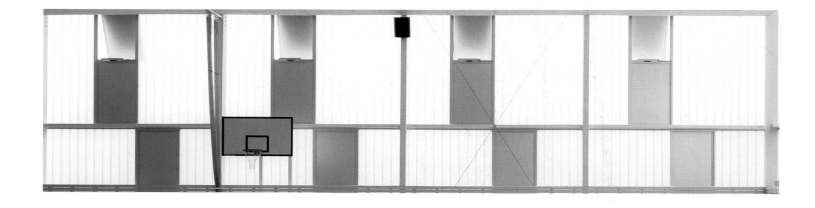

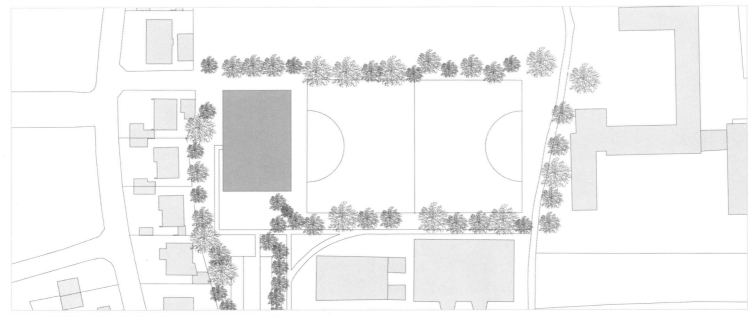

The sports- hall (30 m x 45 m x 8 m) is used both by the neighbouring High School and of local sportsclub.

© Fink + Jocher

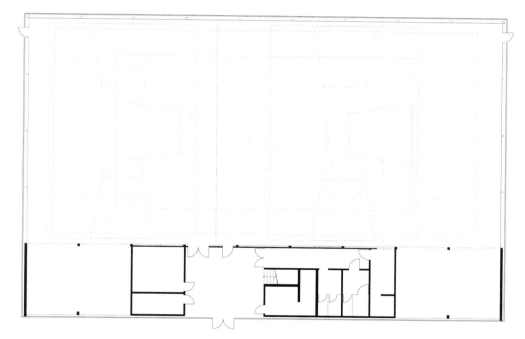

Ground floor

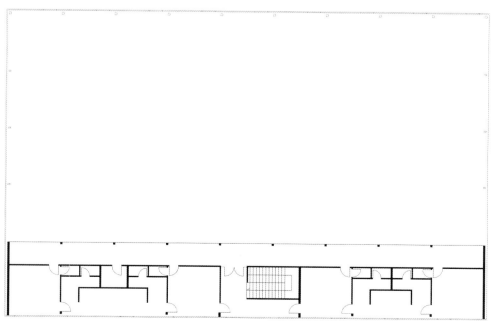

First floor

211

North elevation

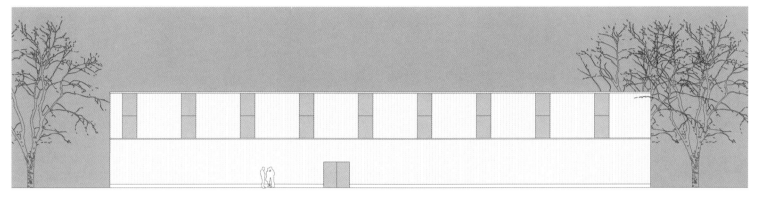

South elevation

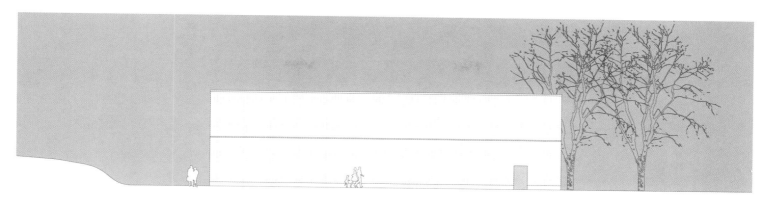

East elevation

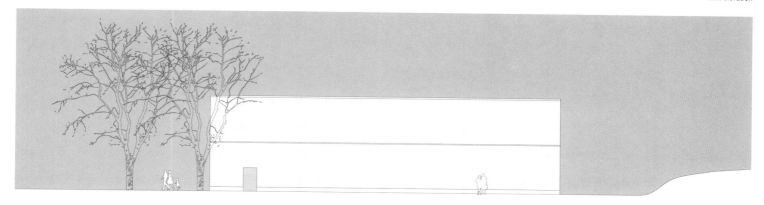

West elevation

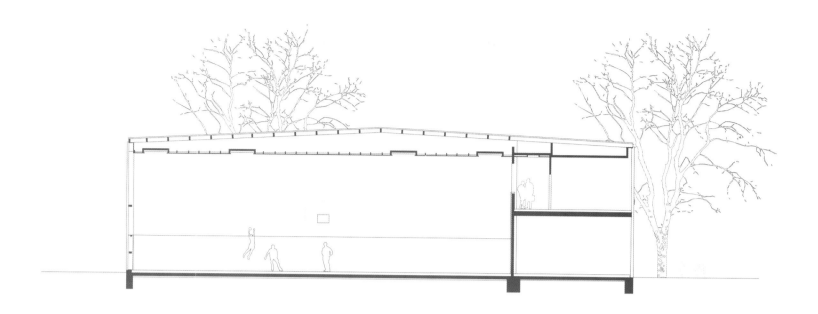

The external sealing is made from glass with translucent thermal insulation that protects the court from overheating.

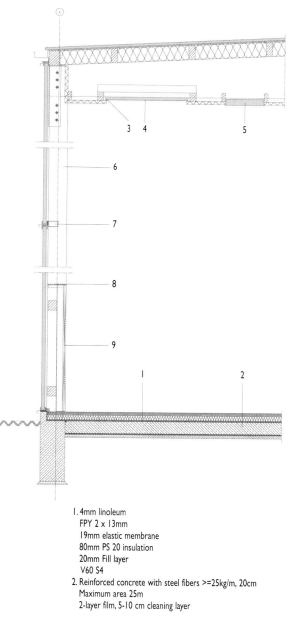

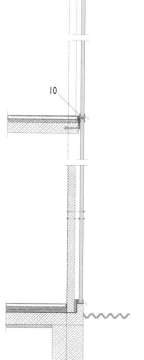

1. 4mm linoleum
   FPY 2 x 13mm
   19mm elastic membrane
   80mm PS 20 insulation
   20mm Fill layer
   V60 S4
2. Reinforced concrete with steel fibers >=25kg/m, 20cm
   Maximum area 25m
   2-layer film, 5-10 cm cleaning layer

3. Ventilation grille
4. Electric radiator
5. Lighting
6. 16/30cm stanchion
7. 180 x 100 x 7.1 RR
8. Perforated sheet
9. 46mm reflecting wall
10. Elastic coupling

Vincen Cornu

Dojo in Artenay

Artenay, France

Photographs: Contributed by the architect

This project is located near the outer limit of the town of Artenay, and the increasingly unusual circumstance of a clear demarcation between town and fields led the architects to emphasize the building's connection with the countryside. The structure and materials reflect the energy of rural architecture, with its direct, strong, generous and often beautiful form of expression.

The building is simple, oriented East-West, with a clear and direct structure, and uses solid, natural materials without any veneer effects.

The main structure is made of Douglas pine wood, which conserves its natural appearance, on a base of reinforced concrete rising to a maximum of 20 cm from the ground.

The window frames are made of wood, and the large windows are protected from the sunlight and other external elements by horizontal wooden elements. The opaque parts of the façade are made from prefabricated VIROC sections, painted off-white.

The solid elements generate voids between the building and its neighboring building, and these negative spaces are just as important to the design as the solids. The project is woven into the urban fabric, with walls articulating, containing and framing the voids.

The roof is made of two inclined surfaces (42°), resembling the slope of traditional Artenay barns. As with other local buildings, the roof has no drainpipes and the rainwater is gathered on the ground by gutters. The roof covering is made of zinc, and each side includes two horizontal projections to provide light and ventilation.

Like the exterior, the main interior space is large and barn-like with a visible structure, and filled with natural light.

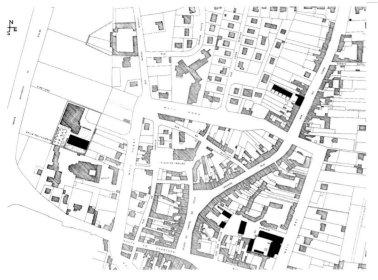

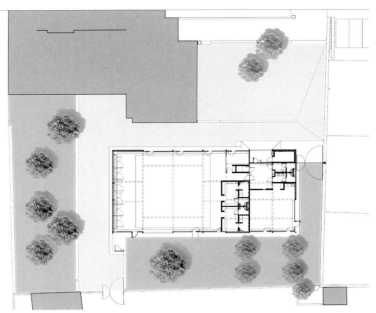

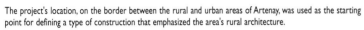
The project's location, on the border between the rural and urban areas of Artenay, was used as the starting point for defining a type of construction that emphasized the area's rural architecture.

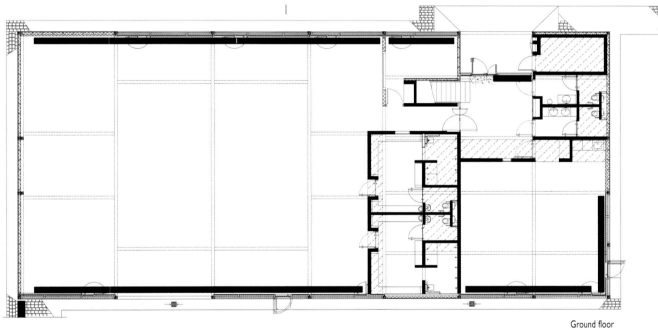

Ground floor

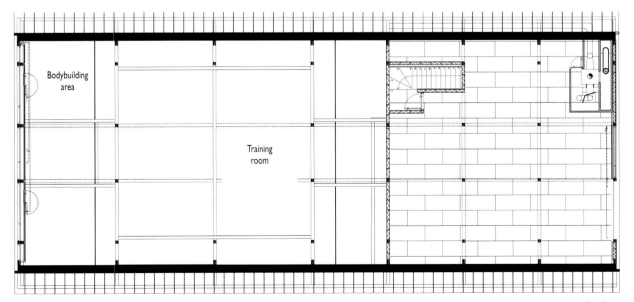

Bodybuilding area

Training room

First floor

221

The inspiration for the structure and materials can be found in the local rural architecture: in fact, the building's external appearance is similar to traditional barns in the area.

East elevation

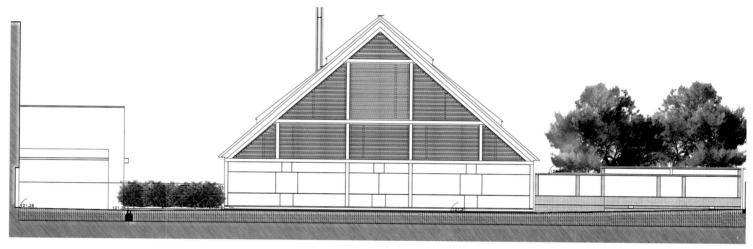

West elevation

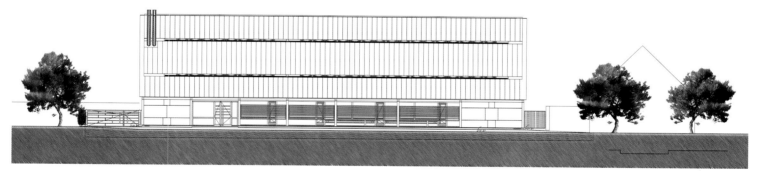

North elevation

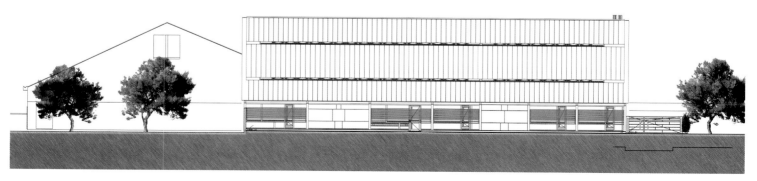

South elevation

The visible structure is made of Douglas pine, conserving its natural appearance, and rests on a concrete base. The opaque parts of the facade consist of prefabricated VIROC panels painted white, and all the finishes are made from natural materials.

1. VIROC panel
2. Light and ventilation opening
3. Zinc roof covering
4. Plastering
5. Reinforced concrete base
6. Rainwater drainage
7. Window: wooden frame
8. Sunlight protection: wooden lamellae

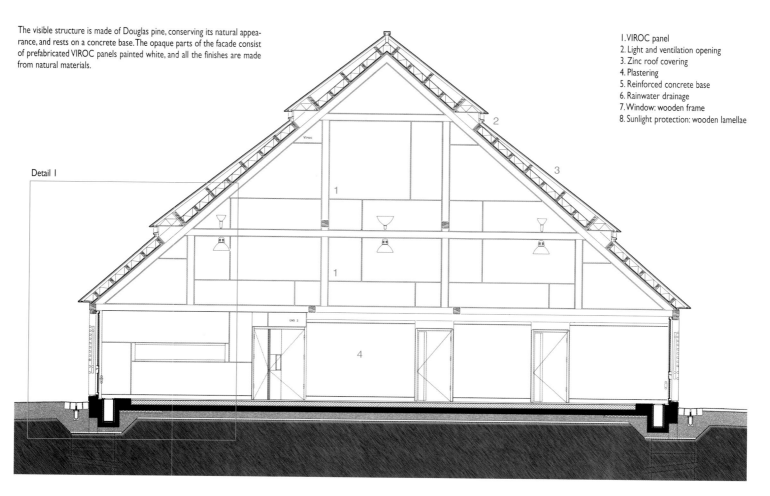

Detail 1

Detail 1, elevation and section

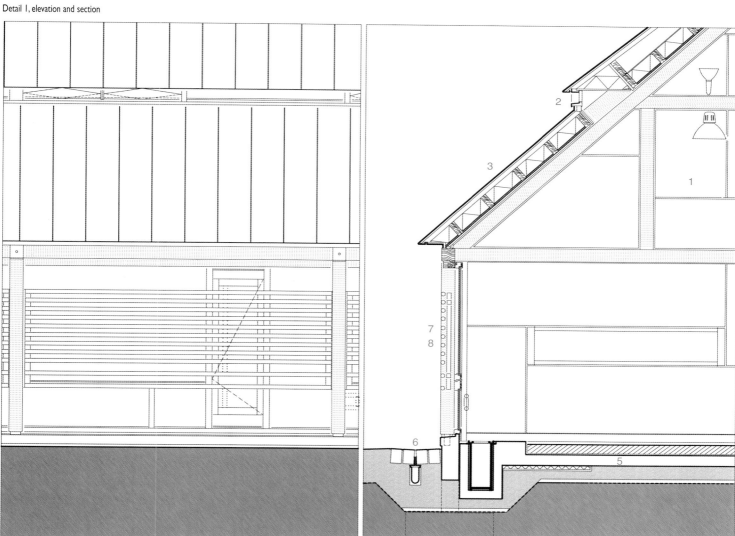

Leeb & Grundmann Architects

Gymnasium at the school of St. Margarethen

Wolfsberg, Austria

Photographs: Paul Ott

The local primary school's need for a new gymnasium was the perfect opportunity to implement a larger project that would house a few local sports clubs and provide facilities to hold national competitions in the small village of St Margarethen. The school is embedded in a rural setting, surrounded by old farm buildings and framed by gently sloping hills and forests, and the size of the new gymnasium made it a relatively major intervention in the rural fabric. In order to create a building that would adapt to the proportion of existing village buildings, the architects used landscaping strategies as an important basis of the project, and the whole structure was buried into the ground as far as the local soil conditions allowed.

From the outside, the gymnasium appears as a box shape tilted up towards the distant hills. This box is partially expressed as a raised volume with a glazed cut separating the lower part. The rest of the volumes are of lower height, in order to adapt to the surroundings. The entire façade on the lower level is glazed and can be opened up in order to provide natural ventilation, and the exterior seems to flow into the space of the gymnasium.

The project included turning the existing gymnasium, located in the school basement, into locker rooms and showers. The basement floor level was raised and evened out in order to provide easier access to the playing field, with a ramp connecting the ground floor of the school with the visitor level of the gymnasium.

The main entrance to the visitor level is reached by passing through a sloping tunnel that projects beyond the existing building, so that it is visible from the street. The indoor playing field is flanked by visitors galleries placed at an angle, with the main gallery representing the spatial continuation of the entrance tunnel and leading onto the visitors terrace.

The roof structure is formed by a system of custom-made steel beams that rest of specially shaped concrete columns, which also carry angular prefabricated concrete parts that cover the main visitors gallery. On the northern side the steel beams are supported by a system of slanted slim steel columns. An expressive hung ceiling made of wood slats follows the contour of the steel beams, adding to the dynamic appearance of the space.

The design and materials used in this gymnasium represent a conscious approach towards interacting with a rural setting, without betraying contemporary notions of space and construction methods.

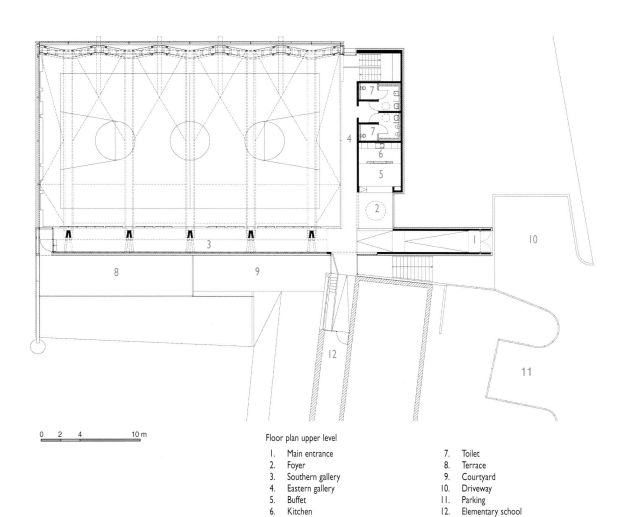

0 2 4   10 m

Floor plan upper level

1.	Main entrance	7.	Toilet
2.	Foyer	8.	Terrace
3.	Southern gallery	9.	Courtyard
4.	Eastern gallery	10.	Driveway
5.	Buffet	11.	Parking
6.	Kitchen	12.	Elementary school

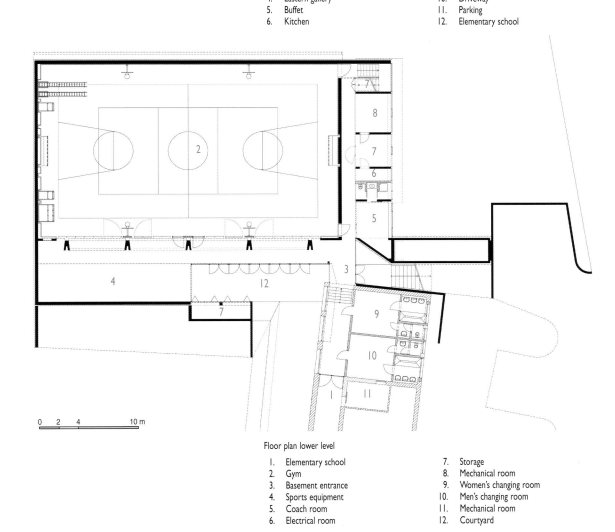

0 2 4   10 m

Floor plan lower level

1.	Elementary school	7.	Storage
2.	Gym	8.	Mechanical room
3.	Basement entrance	9.	Women's changing room
4.	Sports equipment	10.	Men's changing room
5.	Coach room	11.	Mechanical room
6.	Electrical room	12.	Courtyard

In keeping with the desire to integrate the overall project into its environment, the ground of the northern part of the outdoor playing field was adjusted to form two approaches: one sloping down to a small courtyard providing access to the lower level, the other sloping up to the visitors entrance.

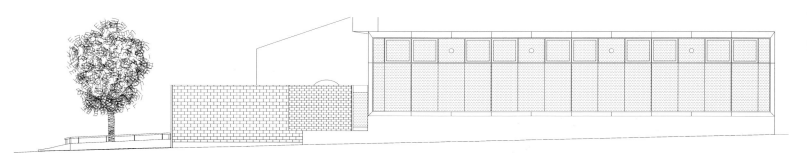

North Elevation

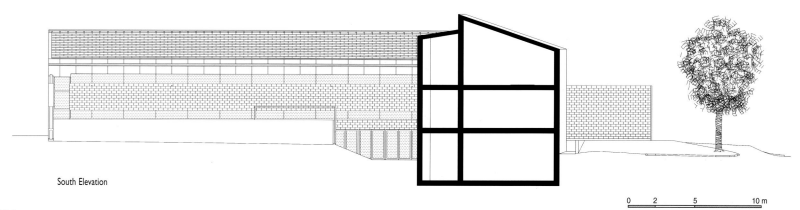

South Elevation

0   2   5   10 m

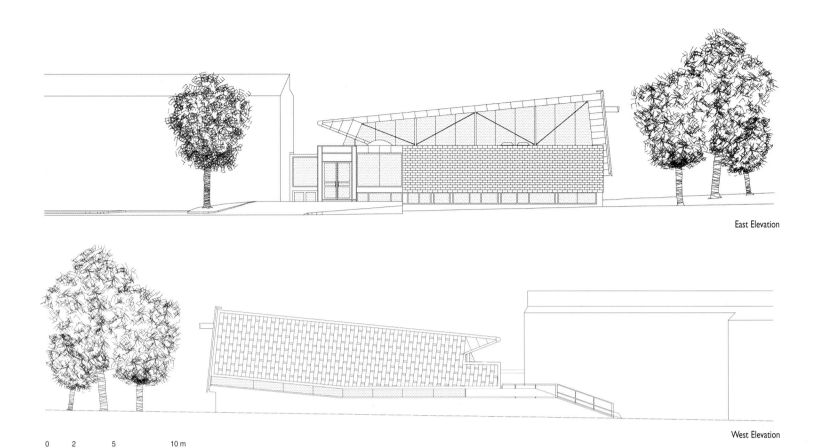

East Elevation

West Elevation

0   2   5   10 m

The box shape is covered with copper shingles, while the rest of the building is finished in gray bitumen shingles and the base is finished in dark gray stucco. The dark colors and the use of copper are part of a design strategy focused on respecting the rural environment.

235

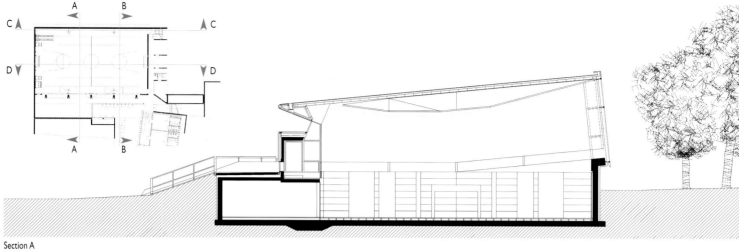

Section A

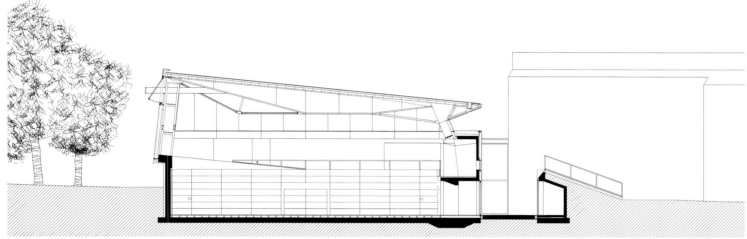

Section B

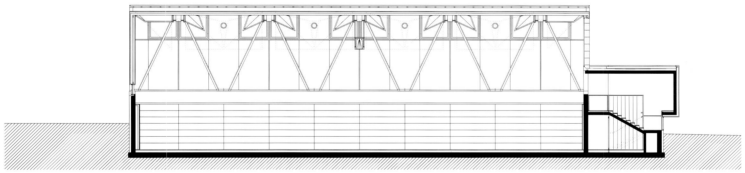

Section C

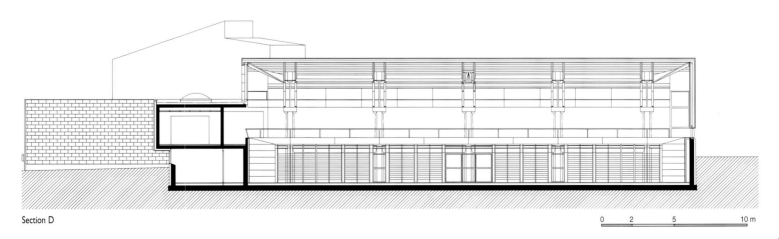

Section D

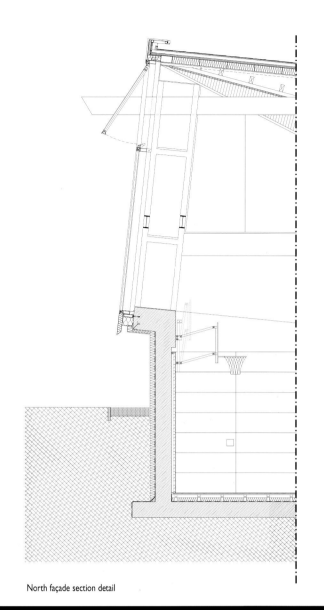

North façade section detail

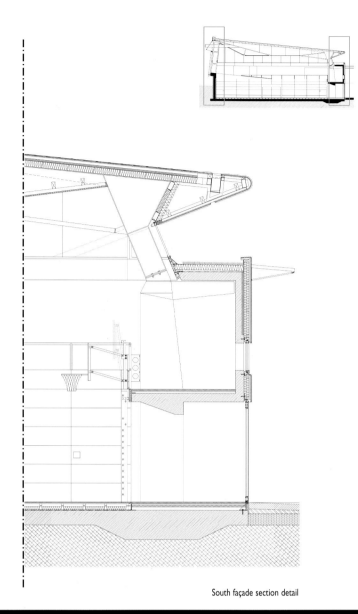

South façade section detail

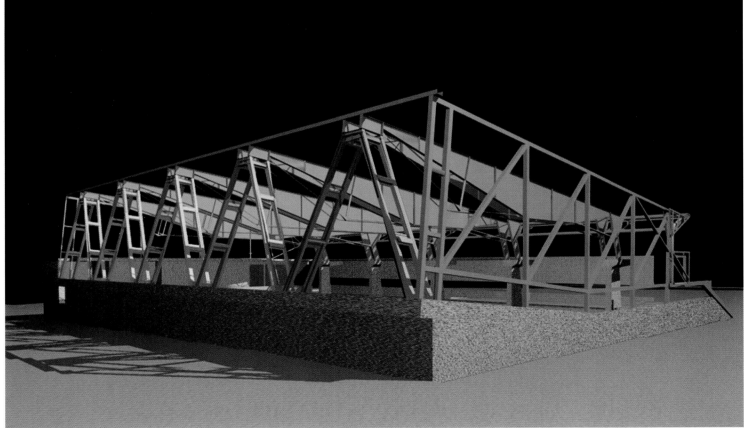